CW00925969

CURING
AFFLUENZA
HOW TO BUY LESS STUFF AND SAVE THE WORLD

CURING AFFLUENZA

HOW TO BUY LESS STUFF AND SAVE THE WORLD

Richard Denniss

Published by Black Inc.,
an imprint of Schwartz Publishing Pty Ltd
Level 1, 221 Drummond Street
Carlton VIC 3053, Australia
enquiries@blackincbooks.com
www.blackincbooks.com

Copyright © Richard Denniss 2017
Richard Denniss asserts his right to be known as the author of this work.

ALL RIGHTS RESERVED.
No part of this publication may be reproduced, stored in a retrieval system,
or transmitted in any form by any means electronic, mechanical, photocopying,
recording or otherwise without the prior consent of the publishers.

National Library of Australia Cataloguing-in-Publication entry:
Denniss, Richard, author.
Curing affluenza: how to buy less stuff and save the world/
Richard Denniss.
9781863959414 (paperback)
9781925435771 (ebook)
Consumption (Economics) –Moral and ethical aspects.
Quality of life.
Materialism – Psychological aspects.
Consumer behavior.

Cover and text design by Tristan Main

Printed and bound in Great Britain by Clays Ltd, St Ives plc

FSC
www.fsc.org
MIX
Paper from
responsible sources
FSC® C018072

Contents

Preface

My father remembers folding up the brown-paper bag that had contained his school lunch. There was no reason he couldn't use it again the next day. So he did. To this day my parents' kitchen drawer contains a ball of rubber bands that found their way into the house, often wrapped around junk mail. 'Why would you throw perfectly good rubber bands away?' ask my parents.

I throw perfectly good rubber bands away. I resent the people who ignore my requests for no junk mail to be left at my house, but I don't stockpile the rubber bands they give me. I grew up in a house where we were never short of rubber bands. My parents didn't. Culture shapes behaviour.

Just as a fish can't taste the water it swims in, it is hard for citizens in affluent societies to notice just how weird their culture has become. Culture tells us when it is time to swap the clothes we have for some new ones, to swap our car for a new one, and even when to rip out a perfectly functional kitchen and replace it with a 'modern' one. It is cultural preference, rather than the price of seed, that has made lawn the largest irrigated crop in the US, and it is culture that tells us it's more convenient to drive to the shops to buy vegetables than to plant them in the land taken up by our lawns.

Our culture also encourages us to throw away perfectly useful things, made of scarce natural resources, to send the signal that we aren't stingy, mean or, worst of all, poor. Each year the citizens of rich countries throw away mountains of perfectly edible food, perfectly wearable clothes and fitness equipment that has never been used. Yet many of those doing the wasting feel poor, and many believe that if they throw the things they buy in the recycling bin, or leave them with a charity, their waste is actually a form of generosity.

We have built a culture where buying things is increasingly unrelated to using things. And we have built a culture where things are thrown away not because they are broken, but because they send the wrong signal about who we are. We use material things for primarily symbolic reasons, which means we throw them out not when they are broken, but when we need to send a new signal. In turn we have built the most materially wealthy communities the world has ever known, but despite this abundance of stuff, our culture makes people feel that they never have enough, or the right, stuff.

Our culture is suffering from a bad case of affluenza. Despite the incredible increase in material production and consumption over the past century, many of the richest people in the richest countries feel poor. But it needn't be this way. This culture that impoverishes us is a new one. It wasn't the norm when my dad was at school. By the time I was at school things were changing, and I think they have accelerated rapidly in recent years.

So if affluenza hasn't always been with us, and isn't uniformly spread across all countries, then obviously we can reduce or even eradicate it if we want to. And that is, of course, the big question: do we want to?

All rich cultures must grapple with what to do with their affluence. Egyptians once built great pyramids, Chinese once built a Great Wall, and in the 1960s and 1970s Americans built a vast nuclear weapons capacity. If we stopped dedicating so much time and so many natural resources to building mountains of wasted stuff, we could do anything we wanted. Of course we couldn't do everything we wanted – we would have to make choices. But instead of being encouraged to question our national goals and make those choices, we are told that the market holds all the answers.

This book argues that markets can no more tell us where to head than a compass can tell a sailor where to sail. Markets are a means towards some ends, but they are silent about the ends that a democratic society should pursue.

This book also argues that, far from encouraging efficiency, markets have become the major driver of waste and inefficiency in developed countries. If we do away with the need to produce mountains of wasted resources, it will be simple to change our society in ways that will reduce the harm we do to the natural environment, improve our quality of life, create more jobs with more meaning and, most of all, give us more time to spend with the people, and on the things, we love the most.

Put simply, curing affluenza means that we will waste far less time and far fewer resources, and in turn make far more of the things we really want more of.

How, then, do we cure affluenza? I don't have all the answers. I don't know what the world will look like in ten years' time, or a hundred. But I do know what I want to see more of and what I want to see less of.

The purpose of this book is to help widen our range of options and, I hope, make people more confident in demanding the changes they want. Most of the following chapters contain case studies, written by diverse authors, that show how individuals and communities have called for, and delivered, change: in their community, in their country and across the globe. The purpose of these case studies is to highlight that change doesn't just happen and isn't only driven by 'the market'. People and communities demand and drive change all the time. There are alternatives, and the more people demand them, the faster change will occur.

The sooner we set out to build new alternatives, the quicker the idea that wasting stuff makes the economy strong will seem as ridiculous as the idea that sacrificing goats or virgins is a good way to improve a harvest.

We don't just need to 'reframe the debate' or 'reform' our policies. We need to fundamentally reshape the economy. History says it's been done before, and voters around the world clearly believe that it is time we did it again.

1.

Diagnosing the Disease

Affluenza is that strange desire we feel to spend money we don't have to buy things we don't need to impress people we don't know.

Affluenza has not only transformed the size of our shopping malls and the contents of our garbage dumps, it has also transformed our culture, environment and economy. And despite the large wealth gap between developed and developing countries, this disease of affluence is 'trickling down' to less well-off countries far more rapidly than the affluence itself. And nothing keeps people poorer than a bad case of affluenza.

Can affluenza be stopped? Like all pandemics, it is easily spread and mutates frequently, so it will be hard to cure. But hard doesn't mean impossible. Surely curing affluenza can't be as hard as wiping out polio with worldwide vaccination, or landing a man on the moon in a rocket that took a decade to build?

But just say we did abandon the idea that wasting resources is good for the economy. Wouldn't the global economic system grind to a halt? Put another way, isn't speeding up the rate at which middle-class people throw away perfectly functional furniture and appliances a good way to create jobs and reduce world poverty?

This book sets out to show several things: that affluenza is economically inefficient, that it is the root cause of environmental destruction, and that it worsens global inequality. If – and this is a big if – we are interested in avoiding climate change, distributing resources more equally and improving the wellbeing of billions of people (rich and poor), then it is essential to wipe out the plague of affluenza.

Many of the world's biggest problems are symptoms of this plague. Rather than treat the symptoms, it is time we tackled the underlying disease.

IT'S THE CULTURE, STUPID

In recent decades, the need for *cultural* change has taken a back seat to debates about evidence-based policy solutions and new technologies. It seems nearly every environmentalist knows that we need a carbon price to fix climate change, for instance, and every social justice campaigner knows that we need more aid money to fix global inequality. But could our focus on such partial measures, worthy as they are, have distracted us from addressing the root cause of these problems? That is, what if it is the brand-new culture of wasteful materialism – which has only emerged in recent decades – that is the major cause of our large social, economic and environmental woes? And what if that same culture is the major barrier to solving them?

This book is not seeking to add a new problem to our global to-do list. Rather, it argues that if we are to fix many of the problems on that list, we need to go up a level in our analysis, examine the cause of multiple problems and solve them simultaneously. In other words, rather than arguing among ourselves about whether global poverty or climate change is the more urgent problem, we need to unite and change the cultural settings that cause both.

Culture doesn't just drive consumer preferences, it also drives our ideas about what is 'politically realistic', 'affordable given current budget realities' and 'economically responsible'. The United States' exit from NAFTA, the United Kingdom's Brexit, and Australia's plans to subsidise construction of the world's largest export coalmine – all of these have nothing to do with shifts in economic theory or changes in technology. They reflect changes in culture and society. This is not to suggest that debates about individual policy ideas aren't useful or important, but it is to say that, by themselves, policy debates are not nearly enough.

Take cars, for example. When the automobile was invented, the law in both the United States and the United

Kingdom required cars to be preceded by someone on foot who had to wave a red flag to alert pedestrians on crowded streets to the oncoming danger. Without public willingness to turn over roads to the drivers of cars, our cities would not look anything like they do today. While technological change made the mass production of cars possible, it was cultural change that made it profitable.

While technological change offers new ways to address old problems, it also offers new ways to cause new problems. It was not scientists or engineers who convinced hundreds of millions of people that driving a two-tonne SUV is the best way to move around a city. Similarly, whether genetic modification is used to cure disease or to clone human beings is a cultural question, not a scientific or economic one.

How we value things is cultural too. Economics textbooks often discuss the paradox that while humans can't live without water, water is cheap, and while we can easily live without diamonds, diamonds are expensive. The answer – for the authors of first-year economics textbooks, at least – lies in the notion of *scarcity*. While water is essential, it is also abundant, and while diamonds are rarely useful (unless you want to make drill bits or saw blades), they are scarce. Price reflects the interaction of usefulness (demand) and scarcity (supply).

But, as so often, the first-year economics textbooks ignore the more interesting question: what makes a thing seem scarce in the first place? Far from being abundant and cheap, bottled water is more expensive than petrol. Indeed, despite the obvious economic inefficiency, cultural norms have made it profitable to ship bottled water from Fiji to the United States, and from France to Australia. That's a paradox worthy of closer examination. Unfortunately for economics students and the wider community, the fundamental role of advertising and marketing in shaping culture and inventing the absurd notion of 'luxury water', and then making it seem scarce, is typically ignored. But if we can get people to spend so much on bottled water, it is surely not impossible to convince them to pay for stylish solar panels or cool electric cars.

The simplest version of economics teaches students – and politicians – that rational people only care about money, and that, when offered a choice between two similar products, the rational consumer will nearly always buy the cheaper one. By contrast, the simplest version of marketing teaches that there is nothing rational about consumers, and that – because most people would prefer to have more status, not less – when offered a choice between two similar products, the real-life human nearly always buys the more prestigious one.

I know, I know, dear reader – you would never be so crass. But imagine your brother-in-law and sister-in-law in the following situations ...

Your brother-in-law has just moved house and is hosting a birthday party for his thirteen-year-old son, with all his new classmates and their parents invited. While out buying supplies, your brother-in-law is standing in the soft-drink section, choosing between Coke, Pepsi and budget 'no-name' cola. Realising that no-name cola is a tenth of the price of Coke or Pepsi, he does the rational thing and buys it. Doesn't he?

Your sister-in-law has just got a new job and is invited to dinner by her new boss. She thinks she should take a bottle of wine, and, not being much of a wine drinker herself, chooses the cheapest wine in the liquor store. Doesn't she?

The fact that *some* people *sometimes* shop on price for *some* products has been turned by the authors of economics textbooks into the 'law of demand', which says that whenever the price of something falls, if all other things remain equal, people will buy more of it. But in the real world, cultural changes have far more impact than price on the demand for most goods and services.

Take beer, for example. An economics textbook might teach students that demand for beer is set by price. A good economics teacher might emphasise that the belief that price is the main determinant of beer consumption depends on the assumption of *ceteris paribus* – Latin for 'all else remaining equal'. But it is a rare economics student (or politician) who picks up that 'all else remaining equal' is code for 'let's assume that social norms, regulation, the distribution of income and the availability of other products won't ever change'.

In reality, because culture and the pursuit of status matter to many people, they may actually prefer to buy expensive imported beer rather than cheap beer, even if the only thing about it that is actually imported is the sticker on the bottle. And even if that beer has been shunned in its home country in favour of imported beer from somewhere else.

For many people in many cultures, the consumption of beer is a sign of either high status (possibly signalling masculinity, especially while watching sport) or low status (possibly signalling poor education, when ordered in a fancy restaurant). And then there is regulation. In most countries the demand for beer is heavily influenced by restrictions on where alcohol can be sold, where it can be consumed, to whom it can be sold, how it can be advertised and what sanctions are imposed on drunken behaviour or drink-driving. The idea that markets are all about price, and that changing the price of something is the best way to change the consumption of that thing, is so partial as to be seriously misleading. Culture matters.

CULTURAL CHANGE AND ECONOMIC CHANGE ARE COMPLEMENTS, NOT SUBSTITUTES

Most people think chips taste better with salt. But if they had to choose between a bowl of unsalted chips and a bowl of salt, plenty would probably opt to eat neither. When they are combined, however, we can't stop eating them! Like many things, salt and potato chips complement each other. Even though economists understand *complementary* goods, economic analysis is much better suited to understanding *substitution*. In turn, economists often imply that the price of salt, not the availability of chips, is the major determinant of how much salt we eat.

Those who want to change the world are right to be appalled by the way government subsidies and permission to freely dump billions of tonnes of carbon dioxide in the atmosphere keeps the price of coal-fired electricity artificially low. But the conclusion that the best way to reduce greenhouse-gas emissions is to introduce a carbon tax and then 'let the market fix the problem' reflects a fundamental misunderstanding of the role of culture in shaping what the market does, and why different people in different countries use vastly different amounts of electricity to perform the same tasks. It also ignores the cultural – and political – question of why so many governments are so keen to spend so much of taxpayers' money subsidising coalmining, oil exploration and the construction of coal-fired power stations in the first place.

The wasteful production and consumption of stuff that is barely or never used causes enormous environmental harm and is a major driver of greenhouse-gas emissions. In turn, tackling global problems such as climate change must, in part at least, involve cultural change to transform the inefficient and environmentally harmful patterns of behaviour that we have come to take for granted.

Just as it was the cultural change of women entering the labour market that drove the growth of commercial childcare, it is the cultural change in favour of wasteful consumption that has driven the enormous growth in the production and disposal of stuff.

This book is not a plea for self-sacrifice. Nor is it an attack on the morality or rationality of the billions of people who spend little (if any) time thinking about how to prevent climate change or reduce global inequality. Consumers around the world have not consciously set out to harm the environment; they have merely made decisions that seem sensible to them in the culture they have inherited, based on the information they have been given. Just as people who have been exposed to the influenza virus can't be blamed for catching it, people who have been brought up in a culture that encourages wasteful consumption cannot be blamed for their eagerness to replace last year's coolest gadget with this year's. Anyone who wants to change the behaviour of billions of people must focus on reshaping the context in which individual decisions are made. Luckily, such a task is likely easier, and the answers often much closer to home, than many people imagine.

Cultural and consumer change is not rare: it is a permanent feature of our society. Everyone knows someone who, although they once said they would never buy a mobile phone or shop online, now can't stop shopping for things on their smartphone. Everyone knows someone who once said they would never go on a cruise ship or a group holiday, and who swore they would never abandon the daily newspaper for its online equivalent, who has now done so. While there is no doubt that in the past few decades technology and advertising have been the driving force of rapid cultural change, there is also no doubt that communities, churches and governments play a significant role as well.

Culture has an enormous effect on what we do and how we do it. The fact that hundreds of millions of Catholics eat fish on Friday has nothing to do with the price of fish. After the Fukushima nuclear reactor disaster, the Japanese government persuaded commercial office buildings to use less energy for air conditioning, by such measures as encouraging men to take off their jackets in the workplace.

While it is possible to ban smoking in schools, the eating of whale meat, opening shopping centres on a Sunday and using cars in the inner city, most cultural change is incremental and voluntary, not rapid and regulated. Those who want to stop the spread of affluenza need to focus on creating smarter, more attractive patterns of behaviour, rather than chiding people for their current conduct and consumption patterns.

There need be no trade-off between the health of the environment, a more equal distribution of wealth, and the strength of the economy. On the contrary, the pursuit of 'a strong retail sector' based on the premature disposal of perfectly functional goods harms not just the environment, but the economy too.

Consider the following: if everyone disposed of their refrigerator and bought a new one each year, there is no doubt that measured economic activity would increase. But the notion that this surge in refrigerator production and consumption equals a strong economy is absurd.

A culture that encourages rapid increases in the production and consumption of appliances wastes the time and money of its citizens, and drives the cost of living up and the quality of family life down – all while wasting scarce natural resources. Such a culture might boost the profits of those who sell whitegoods, but this sort of churning, like the rapid heartbeat of a sick patient, is an indicator of a stressed system, not a strong one.

THERE ARE MANY ALTERNATIVES

We are surrounded by alternative ways to organise our communities and economies. The 195 countries of the world present a vast array of choices about how to structure a society and shape an economy. Within countries, different states and cities make vastly different decisions about the kinds of services to provide, the amount of these services to provide and the way in which those services will be developed. In 7000 years of recorded history, communities have tried anarchy, communism and everything in between.

Margaret Thatcher once declared that There Is No Alternative to free-market capitalism, but her own Conservative Party recently backed Brexit, the UK's withdrawal from Europe's free exchange of people and products. While those with ulterior motives might like to pretend otherwise, history, geography and economics make clear that we are surrounded by alternatives. It's not finding alternatives that is hard, it is agreeing on them.

Choosing national goals is a cultural question with significant economic consequences. The claim that there is no alternative to Thatcher's vision is tantamount to saying that there is no alternative to Thatcher's preferred cultural norms and goals. Modern and ancient history show how wrong she was. The pyramids and the Great Wall of China were built long before anyone knew how to measure gross domestic product (GDP). The Roman Empire was built without reference to GDP. The Industrial Revolution, the invention of the aeroplane and the electrification of cities all predate the ability of national statistical offices to tell us how fast an economy is growing. The mass mobilisation of economic resources during World War I and World War II was achieved without quarterly data on economic growth.

So the idea that 'there is no alternative' to our current obsession with maximising the dollar value of stuff that is bought and sold (that is, maximising the rate of GDP growth) is as ridiculous historically as it is absurd economically. For all but seventy of the 7000 years of recorded history, kings, emperors, prime ministers and presidents have had to manage their countries' affairs without recourse to regular economic statistics. In fact, those who governed before we came up with the idea of GDP found it easier to make big investments in their country's future than the current generation of politicians, who seem obsessed by this one statistic.

None of this is to say that the limitations of GDP are the cause of the world's problems. On the contrary, the fault lies not with the statistic but with its misuse by those who should know better. One of the fathers of GDP, Simon Kuznets, once observed that 'the welfare of a nation can scarcely be inferred from a measure of national income'. More poetically, the former US senator Robert F. Kennedy said four decades ago:

> The gross national product does not allow for the
> health of our children, the quality of their education
> or the joy of their play. It does not include the beauty
> of our poetry or the strength of our marriages, the
> intelligence of our public debate or the integrity of
> our public officials. It measures neither our wit nor
> our courage, neither our wisdom nor our learning,
> neither our compassion nor our devotion to our

country. It measures everything, in short, except that which makes life worthwhile.

Although those who invented GDP were adamant it should not be used as a measure of progress, many national leaders do exactly that. And just as building big pyramids had major consequences for the shape of the Egyptian economy and the wellbeing of Egypt's people, the goal of maximising GDP has had major consequences for our society, economy and natural environment. But there is nothing economic about the selection of these goals. The choice to pursue GDP growth, pyramid construction, the building of a Great Wall or colonial expansion is a cultural choice, not an economic one. While cultural choices have economic consequences, it is important to realise that they are not economic choices with cultural consequences.

As the refrigerator example shows, there is also no evidence to suggest that the pursuit of GDP growth and the pursuit of economic efficiency are one and the same thing. There are many reasons that a community, a country or a planet might want to be cured of affluenza. For instance, if we abandon the idea that the more stuff we produce and dispose of, the richer we will be, this could significantly reduce human pressure on the natural environment. But that does not *necessarily* follow. Perhaps future generations will seek to stop wasting resources pursuing consumerism in order to free up resources to build more pyramids, enormous armies or fleets of space-ships to take us to the stars.

Whatever goals a culture settles on, to insist that 'there is no alternative' is absurd from the point of view of both history and economics. New norms, new cultures and new ways to buy and sell things will always develop. And as the re-emergence of vinyl records reminds us, old norms are only ever a cultural change away.

SO WHAT SHOULD WE DO?

There is nothing in any economics textbook to tell us what our national goals should be. While talk of maximising growth, balancing the budget, increasing exports and improving national security all sound like answers to the question 'What should we do?', they aren't. They tell us nothing about what we think we need more of, what we think we can do with less of, and how the benefits of production should be distributed.

One of the many problems with the recent obsession with the *size* of GDP is that it has silenced debate about the *shape* of GDP. Do we want our economy to build homes for the homeless, or holiday homes for the holiday-homeless? Do we want our economy to produce more fresh food, or more junk food? Do we want to see more investment in renewable energy, or more in coal-fired power stations?

Do we want more cars on our streets, or more trains running under them?

These important questions about the shape of our economy have been framed as somehow secondary to the question of how big we want our economy to be. Following this logic, we should ask people how much food they would like for dinner before we ask them what kind of food they would like.

Ironically, economics actually has many useful tools for a debate about what shape economy we would like to build in the coming decades. Indeed, a foundational principle of economics is that every time scarce resources are used to produce one thing, we give up the opportunity to produce something else. This is the concept of the 'opportunity cost'.

Just as the resources dedicated to the construction of Egypt's pyramids could have been dedicated to the construction of roads, dams, houses or fortifications, so too the resources dedicated to kitchen renovations and unused exercise equipment could have been dedicated to public transport or increased leisure time. Former US president Dwight D. Eisenhower said it best:

> Every gun that is made, every warship launched,
> every rocket fired signifies, in the final sense, a theft
> from those who hunger and are not fed, those who
> are cold and are not clothed. This world in arms is not
> spending money alone. It is spending the sweat of its

labourers, the genius of its scientists, the hopes of its
children. The cost of one modern heavy bomber is
this: a modern brick school in more than thirty cities.
It is two electric power plants, each serving a town
of 60,000 population. It is two fine, fully equipped
hospitals. It is some fifty miles of concrete pavement.
We pay for a single fighter with a half-million bushels
of wheat. We pay for a single destroyer with new
homes that could have housed more than 8000 people.

Do we prefer tax cuts, or more spending on education?
Do we want to give more funds to defence, or to public transport? Do we subsidise fossil fuels, or invest in renewable
energy? Such collective decisions have enormous consequences – not just for the rate of economic growth, but for its
shape, distribution and environmental impact – and, most
importantly, for how our culture and society will evolve.

Cultural change is not just important, it is inevitable.
Like technological change, cultural change makes the society and economy of 2117 as impossible for us to predict, or
even to imagine, as it was for someone in 1917 to foresee
middle-class life in 2017.

But while cultural, technological and economic change
is inevitable, the direction of that change is not. Will people in 2117 work more hours than people today, or fewer?
Will income equality within and between countries grow,
or shrink? Will countries spend more money on defence,

or diplomacy? Will they spend more on prisons, or on crime prevention? Will robots be provided by governments to help support disabled people with low incomes? Or will robots create a new army of impoverished and unemployed people?

It is up to individuals, communities and countries to answer the question: 'What shape should our economy be?' While there is no right answer, every answer has clear consequences. The existence of scarce resources means that everybody cannot have everything, especially if everybody wants to have more stuff than everybody else. But the fact that everybody can't have everything doesn't mean that everyone can't have the material wellbeing necessary to pursue their personal, cultural, intellectual, spiritual, sporting or other passions.

My purpose in this book is not to announce what the right choices are, but to broaden the menu from which choices can be made – by individuals, communities and countries. In essence, I am arguing three things:

1. Consumerism – or the love of buying new things – is incredibly economically inefficient, and can be criticised with the same tools of orthodox economics that are usually used to defend it. Wasting resources is not a good way to 'create wealth' or anything except piles of waste.

2. The path to prosperity cannot be paved with discarded appliances that were never used – even if they have been recycled. Rather than shun materialism – or the love

of things – as a form of personal or spiritual weakness that must be overcome, materialism must be encouraged and rewarded. Only when billions of people aspire to cling to the material things they deem necessary for a comfortable life – to cherish them, repair them and hand them on to their friends or children in better condition than they acquired them– will a population of 7.5 billion people be able to tread lightly on the planet.

3. Once we shift the debate from the size of economy we want to the shape of economy we want, then the link between wasteful consumerism and job creation can be severed once and for all. While spending money on things we don't really need is one way to create jobs, spending the same amount of money on infrastructure or services that we actually value will likely create even more jobs. Technology to allow drones to deliver imported products, purchased online, direct to our homes might boost the profits of some retailers, but it will do little to create local jobs. And while the cultural willingness to rapidly dispose of all that home-delivered stuff might make for a 'strong retail sector', the belief that the economic, democratic or military strength of a society is proportionate to the frequency with which its citizens update their mobile phones and toasters is absurd. Curing affluenza will not just strengthen our relationships and our community – avoiding enormous amounts of waste will also reshape, and strengthen, our economy.

IT'S NOT (ALL) ABOUT YOU

> *'How many people ruin themselves by laying out money on trinkets of frivolous utility? What pleases these lovers of toys is not so much the utility, as the aptness of the machines which are fitted to promote it. All their pockets are stuffed with little conveniences.'*

Adam Smith

Like many environmentalists today, Adam Smith, the father of what Margaret Thatcher thought of as free-market economics, bemoaned the way so many people spent so much of their money on trinkets and baubles. But while mocking other people's consumption choices has a long history, such mockery has done little to change consumer behaviour or the wider culture.

Focusing solely on becoming a conscious consumer and minimising your individual ecological footprint will do nothing to stop the construction of the coalmines or coal-fired power stations that cause climate change, or to ensure that new investment is made in renewable energy or public transport. Just as proponents of the status quo like to create false dilemmas to make change harder, those who seek change often create false dilemmas for themselves. Asking ourselves whether it is individual action or political action that is more important is as unhelpful as asking whether we should first tackle world poverty or climate change. Good strategies achieve more than one thing at a time.

The following chapters argue that rapid cultural change requires not just personal and political action, but also personal actions that make political action easier, and political actions that make personal actions easier. Just as culture affects the economy and the economy affects culture, actions at an individual and political level can either reinforce each other or impede each other. Good strategies ensure action at one level makes action at other levels easier.

Most obviously, when individuals opt out of community and democratic campaigns and take themselves 'off-grid', they rob those campaigns of their time and energy. More fundamentally, if those who have chosen to minimise their footprint lose sight of the cultural or financial reasons why most other people are apathetic about or even hostile to change, this can do more to entrench cultural division than to persuade the vast majority that curing affluenza will improve their lives.

Affluenza is a public-health problem that cannot be solved through individual piety. While the behaviour of individuals has a significant role to play, individualistic conceptions of the problem – and of solutions to it – can do more harm than good.

The best way to protect yourself from cholera is to ensure your city invests in well-maintained sewers. The best way to protect yourself from polio is to ensure you live in a country that vaccinates all children against it. The best way to prevent the spread of malaria is to prevent the climate change that will allow the mosquitoes that carry the disease to thrive in cities that are currently too cool to sustain them. Similarly, the best way to protect yourself from the consequences of affluenza is not to take yourself off-grid and start prepping for the apocalypse, but to work effectively, and at multiple levels, to shift the shape of our economy in as many ways as possible.

Blaming those who fell victim to the plague, cholera or AIDS for contracting a contagious disease may have made some people feel morally superior, but it did nothing to prevent the spread of disease. Curing affluenza requires not only a careful diagnosis and the confidence to believe it can be stamped out, but also a willingness among those who can see the problem to work constructively with those who are yet to perceive the threat. When it comes to curing affluenza, it is more important to be effective than to be lauded for being right.

Bob Brown

At the end of the nineteenth century, Tasmania, which began the century powered by convicts, was Australia's poorest colony. However, it had mountains, rivers and lots of rain. In 1895, shortly after a portion of Niagara's waters was captured to light up the night in the US, the waters of Tasmania's

Cataract Gorge were turning turbines to light up the city of Launceston.

In 1916 Tasmania's Great Lake outlet was dammed to send electricity to a zinc-processing factory on the northern outskirts of Hobart and to the capital itself. The air was electric. Hydro-electricity's promise seemed to have no bounds. Reputable pundits were predicting that excess electricity sent charging through farm paddocks would produce bumper crops.

The Hydro-Electric Commission (HEC) began measuring up every river and watercourse in Tasmania for dams. By the 1950s the supply of hydro-electricity exceeded the need, threatening the Commission's engineering elite's raison d'être, so the search was on to attract more heavy industries with the lure of super-cheap electricity. The power was so cheap that the sixteen biggest factories won secret contracts to keep locally owned small businesses and households from wanting similar rates. The price was so secret that no member of parliament even knew what it was. Popular Labor premier 'Electric' Eric Reece espoused turning Launceston's idyllic Tamar Valley into 'the Ruhr of the south'.

Despite a public outcry, the stunningly beautiful Lake Pedder National Park was flooded in 1972 in order to produce a mere 80 megawatts of electricity, when a single coal-fired station from that time could produce ten or twenty times as much. The new dam was to help supply Comalco's aluminium smelter, which consumed one-third of all the HEC's power at less than the cost of production. The pro-HEC mantra was 'jobs, jobs, jobs'.

Premier Reece scoffed at the increasing number of visitors bushwalking in Tasmania as 'mainlanders' who came with one five-pound note and one shirt and went home 'having changed neither'.

However, the decade after the destruction of Lake Pedder, with the introduction of colour television, saw a national awakening of concern for Australia's natural environment, at least in wild and scenic Tasmania. The community campaign to save the Franklin River from the HEC's ongoing dam-building program ultimately succeeded, but it required an immense effort. As Machiavelli had warned four centuries earlier, if you want to change the world, get ready to be crushed by those who already have the power and the money.

Citizens who saw Tasmania's future wellbeing built upon its 'clean, green' assets, including wilderness, wildlife, the world's cleanest air and fresh food and wine (preferably organic), were dismissed as 'sandal-footed do-gooders' back then. At the peaceful blockade of the Franklin dam works, 1500 people were arrested and 500 jailed, myself among them. Amidst HEC warnings of power shortages, economic downturn and job losses (none of these eventuated), it took a national furore, a change of federal government and a High Court verdict to save the wild river in 1983.

In the middle of this pivotal debate over Tasmania's future, the chief of the HEC declared that if the future was to be determined by public opinion 'we are doomed in Tasmania and we are doomed around the world'. HEC supporters had bumper stickers advocating 'Fertilise the southwest (wilderness), doze in a greenie'.

Far from being doomed, the Tasmanian Wilderness World Heritage Area, with the Franklin River flowing free in its heartland, is now internationally renowned as a place of inestimable value. It is the biggest attraction for Tasmania's burgeoning tourism and hospitality industries, which now support many more jobs than the declining mining, logging and dam-building industries combined.

An American outdoors publication recently judged the Franklin number one on its list of the world's ten most desirable whitewater rafting adventures. It was nearly a dam.

Tasmania's mindset has changed almost unimaginably from the dam-building era. The state now markets not just its tourism, but its food, beer, wine and quality of life in terms of its pristine natural environment. Eco-labelling is everywhere. Beer and cheese have Tasmanian tigers and free-flowing mountain rivers on their labels. Fine wines and walking adventures have replaced tailraces and turbines in the island's core imagery. The more than one million annual visitors, rather than being scoffed at, are now welcomed as the generators of a new age of Tasmanian wellbeing.

The HEC has taken to building wind turbines. There are no more dams on its horizon. It now proudly labels itself as 'green'.

These cultural changes, which have driven enormous economic transformation and wealth creation, did not 'just happen'. The market didn't stop the destruction of our natural assets;

the community did. Driving such change was neither easy nor quick, and even today it is challenged by a shrinking, and ageing, minority. But Tasmania's wild rivers, booming tourism industry and whisky judged to be the best in the world are proof that people can take control of the shape of their community and their economy.

Dr Bob Brown helped lead the community campaign against the Franklin River Dam and went on to stand for the world's first green political party, the United Tasmania Group, which evolved into the Australian Greens, which he represented in the Senate from 1996 to 2012. In 1990 he was awarded the US Goldman Environmental Prize.

2.

A Good Dose of Materialism Helps a Bad Case of Affluenza

Affluenza has not just changed the world, it has also changed the way we see the world. Short of money? Borrow some. Caught in the rain? Buy an umbrella. Thirsty? Buy a bottle of water then throw the bottle away. Our embrace of 'convenience' and our acceptance of our inability to plan ahead is an entirely new way of thinking, and over the past seventy years we have built a new and different economic system to accommodate it.

There is nothing inevitable about this current way of thinking, consuming and producing. On the contrary, the vast majority of humans who have ever lived (and the majority of humans alive today) would find the idea of using our scarce resources to produce things that are designed to be thrown away absolutely mad. But the fact that our consumer culture is a recent innovation does not mean it will be easy to change. Indeed, the last few decades have shown how contagious affluenza can be. But we have not always lived this way, which proves that we don't have to persist with it. We can change – if we want to.

For millennia, the ability of humans to survive and thrive was based on our ability to think very differently from the way the average consumer in a modern shopping centre thinks. Affluenza is so entangled with our modern culture that its impact on our words and our thinking can be hard to spot, but think for a moment about the term *shopping centre*. You go to a food market to buy food, and a fitness centre to get fit, so we must go to a shopping centre to get some shopping done, right? We have been acculturated to enjoy the *process*, not the *product*.

The ability to plan ahead – to make sacrifices today that deliver benefits tomorrow – is one of the defining characteristics of intelligence, and one of the main traits of maturity. But that isn't what 'recreational shopping' is about.

A famous experiment involves leaving a young child alone in a room with a marshmallow, with the promise that, if the treat is still there when the experimenter returns to the room, the child will be given two more marshmallows. Kids under three typically eat the marshmallow as soon as the experimenter leaves the room, gaining immediate satisfaction but costing themselves two extra marshmallows. The ability to resist temptation is seen as a developmental milestone, a step along the path to maturity.

Like a kid in a room with a marshmallow, people who rely on borrowed money to buy trinkets today are 'deciding' to buy fewer things tomorrow. A lot fewer. Imagine you cleared $50,000 last year after tax, and spent an extra $10,000 on a credit card, for a total of $60,000 spent over the year. If you keep earning $50,000 the following year, to get back to square one you need to spend around $39,000 – that's $21,000 less than you spent the previous year. That's a cut in spending of more than 30 per cent!

Why is the difference so big? Well, first, you can't keep spending $10,000 more than you earn each year, so you need to cut your spending from $60,000 to $50,000. And then you have to repay the $10,000 credit card balance, which means you only have $40,000 to spend this year. And then you have to pay the credit card interest. Let's be optimistic and assume you only had to pay 10 per cent interest on your $10,000 loan, so that's another $1000 you owe. So after spending $60,000 in the first year, you will only have around $39,000 to spend in the second, or else you will go deeper into debt. That's a $21,000 hit to your lifestyle from one year to the next. That's a lot fewer marshmallows.

You can see why people who accumulate credit card debt often struggle to repay it, especially when they think they need to spend money in order to fit in with friends and colleagues. But that's the plan: the banks and stores offering interest-free periods, loyalty cards and frequent-flyer points are simply giving people a rational-sounding excuse to commit an irrational act. The stores and the banks know that most people won't repay their loans quickly. The banks don't make any money from people who use 'interest-free periods' in the way they are advertised.

We humans didn't just evolve to become more rational and mature as we get older; we also evolved an impulse to adapt to complex social settings. The desire to fit in with our peers is not a weakness but a strength. Those who think only about the costs and benefits of an action to them, and who care nothing about the impact on those around them, often end up working as economists. Everyone wants their kids to fit in and have good social relationships, but, as marketing and political strategists know all too well, the desire to fit in can easily be used against people.

If everyone on your street and in your workplace can afford a new car, why shouldn't you get one too? And if the parents of all your kids' friends can afford to go overseas for a holiday, how come you can't? If everyone else is funding their consumption with borrowed money, they can't all be mad, can they? Culture plays a major role in shaping the choices individuals make. Why else would men wear neckties? Why else would we worry about sending our children to school in outfits that set them apart from kids from all the other schools?

It is no accident that the post–World War II culture of consumerism coincided with the rise of consumer finance; the two phenomena are linked as inextricably as politics and lobbying. The availability of consumer credit helps solve the salesperson's greatest challenge: turning an impulse into an action. Every salesperson knows that closing a sale is much easier when people don't need to walk all the way to the bank and withdraw some cash.

Whether it is the smell of fried food pumped out into the street, the books on display on the footpath out the front of the bookstore, or the colour, lights and sound of the slot machines at a casino, closing the sale for any impulse purchase is much easier when people always have the *capacity* to pay, regardless of their current bank balance.

CONSUMERISM IS THE OPPOSITE OF MATERIALISM

I define *consumerism* as the love of buying things. For some, that means the thrill of hunting for a bargain. For others, it is the quest for the new or the unique. And for others still it is that moment when the shop assistant hands them their new purchase, beautifully wrapped, with a bow, just as though it's a present.

But the love of buying things can, by definition, provide only a transient sense of satisfaction. The feeling can be lengthened by the 'thrill of the chase', and may include an afterglow that includes walking down the street with a new purchase in a branded carry bag. It might even extend to the moment when you get to show your purchase to your friends and family. But the benefits of consumerism are inevitably short-lived as they are linked to the process of the purchase, not the use of the product. So while *consumerism* is the love of buying things, *materialism* is the love of the things themselves – and that's an important distinction.

Salespeople and psychologists are well aware of this phenomenon. The term *buyer's remorse* refers to the comedown that follows the thrill of buying something new. For many, the cold hard light of day takes the gloss off their new gadget, their new shoes or their new car. For some, this can be so overwhelming that they return the item. For a minority, the thrill of buying new things is so great, and the disappointment of owning new things so strong, that they make a habit of buying things they know they will return.

For those interested in the impact of consumption on the natural environment it is crucial to make a clear distinction between the love of buying things and the love of owning things. While *consumerism* and *materialism* are often used interchangeably, taken literally they are polar opposites. If you really loved your car, the thought of replacing it with a new one would be painful. Similarly, if you really loved your kitchen, your belt or your couch, then your *materialism* would prevent you rushing out and buying a new one.

But we have been trained to love the thrill of buying new stuff. We love things not for their material function, but for the symbolic act of acquiring and possessing them – the buzz of anticipating a new thing, of being handed it by a smiling shop assistant, of pulling up at the golf club in an expensive new car. For many, if not most, 'consumers', it is the symbolism of a new handbag or new car, its expensive logo proudly displayed, that delivers happiness, rather than twenty years of using a material object.

It makes no sense to conflate materialism and consumerism. Indeed, our willingness to dispose of perfectly functional material goods and gadgets is the very antithesis of a love of things. The process of buying new things and displaying new symbols might confer status or other psychological benefits, but the pursuit of such symbolic objectives is largely unrelated to the material characteristics of the products being purchased and disposed of.

Symbols matter, and psychological benefits matter. The fact that people are willing to spend their own time and money to show they fit in or to make sure they stand out should be of little or no concern to others. But for those who are concerned with the impact of 7.5 billion humans' consumption decisions on the natural environment, the choice of such symbols matters enormously. Whether people choose to signal their wealth by spending money on huge cars or antique paintings is arbitrary, but that does not mean the environmental consequences aren't highly significant.

Put simply, if we want to reduce the impact on the natural environment of all of the stuff we buy, then we have

to hang on to our stuff for a lot longer. We have to maintain it, repair it when it breaks, and find a new home for it
when we don't need it any longer. If we want to cure affluenza, we have to get more satisfaction from the things we
already own, more satisfaction from services, more satisfaction from leisure time and less satisfaction from the
process of buying new things.

Such a cultural change – from the love of buying to the
love of owning – would radically reshape the economy.
It would reduce the profits of those who sell us stuff for
largely symbolic purposes. Such a cultural change will be
hard to achieve, but surely it can't be as hard as convincing people that commuting to work in cars is convenient,
or that 'recycling' a plastic water bottle after just one use
is sustainable?

WE NEED TO STOP SACRIFICING MATERIAL THINGS FOR SYMBOLIC PURPOSES

Throughout recorded history, making sacrifices has been
important in human culture. Whether it was virgins, slaves,
goats or grain, the idea was pretty much the same: offering
up something valuable to a deity now would deliver greater
benefits in the future.

In rich countries today, billions of tonnes of scarce
natural resources and billions of hours of human effort
are sacrificed in the apparent hope that if we produce

and dispose of enough things, we can 'make the economy strong'.

The idea that the more a society wastes, the wealthier it becomes, is patently absurd. But those who challenge this belief sometimes make the case for change by saying that we need to lower our standard of living, or rein in our lifestyles. That is, those who encourage people to consume, borrow and dispose at a greater rate are promising to make the economy strong, while those encouraging thrift and conservation freely admit that, if their advice is followed, things will get worse! It's not much of a sales pitch.

It would be better to argue that the fewer resources we waste on things we don't really need, the more resources we will have to produce the things we really want. Just as it is absurd to bake a tray of muffins purely to consume the crunchy muffin tops, it is bizarre to spend billions of dollars buying consumer goods we don't need in order to generate a small slice of company-tax revenue, which we can *then* spend on health and education.

Around the world, opinion polls show that people in rich countries can see the problems with the cycle of *work, buy, consume, die*. Just as the link between slaying a goat and next year's rainfall must have appeared tenuous to the average Mayan farmer, the link between wasting lots of stuff and solving poverty appears weak to the average Western consumer, despite all the talk of making the economy strong.

Similarly, repeated surveys across many countries suggest that most people would be happy to have more leisure time and less money, if they could do so without risking their job.

Yet despite these widespread concerns about affluenza, and despite widespread support for the view that cultural change might be desirable, those promoting change often accept – or even celebrate – the argument that reducing our wasteful consumption and increasing our leisure time must result in a worse quality of life. If we are to cure affluenza, we must convince people that they can actually have a much higher material standard of living, and a much less stressful personal life, if they eschew the pursuit of symbolic consumerism and embrace materialism instead.

THE MAIN PURPOSE OF MATERIAL GOODS IS OFTEN SYMBOLIC

In addition to taking pleasure from the act of buying something new (consumerism), a major reason that people throw away perfectly functional things is because they have ceased to perform their symbolic function. That is to say, the things we buy – such as a car, a pair of running shoes or a handbag – can in most cases be seen as performing two entirely separate functions, a material one and a symbolic one.

As every dealer knows, a new car is not just a means of getting from A to B. Even people who buy the cheapest new car they can find know that they could have paid even less if they bought a second-hand car. As well as buying a form of transport, they are simultaneously buying something intangible: status, identity or peace of mind.

For some, the symbolic value of having the latest-model car, the running shoes that the best-paid sportspeople are wearing or the handbag that the most famous celebrity is carrying far outweighs the material purpose served by a car, running shoes or a handbag. In such cases, when a perfectly functional possession ceases to perform its symbolic function well, or at all, it must be replaced. Going out of your way to throw a functional object into the recycling bin is often the last symbolic act for that particular material thing.

The cultural rules that shape such decisions are as complicated as they are contradictory. For example, a man can wear the same dinner suit to countless balls and parties, while a woman who wears the same dress twice feels (often rightly) that she will be criticised.

While wearing antique jewellery might be considered prestigious, 're-gifting' an unused and unwanted Christmas present is often thought to be stingy. Similarly, while a much-loved leather jacket might be appropriate in many settings, suit pants with holes in the knees most likely are not. A pair of ripped denim jeans, on the other hand, can sell at a premium. Symbolism is a complicated but profitable business.

The watch industry has developed a creative response to the apparent dilemma it faces. The sales pitch for a $10,000 watch is that it is a 'timeless' masterpiece that can be handed on to one's children, yet it is hard to sell a lot of watches if customers keep them for decades and hand them on to their children. The solution? Suggest that watch connoisseurs collect a whole array of watches that will last a lifetime.

A THOUGHT EXPERIMENT

Imagine a society in which consumers wore their status on their chests and shoulders in the way that soldiers wear medals and epaulettes. Imagine if we could spend our own money (or borrow other people's) to purchase, quite literally, status symbols. That is, rather than indirectly signal our willingness to spend large amounts of money on clothes, shoes or sports cars in order to send a signal about our income, what if we could simply buy badges with the price we paid for them printed in clear type?

Could it ever happen? Well, car companies make billions of dollars selling near identical cars at quite different prices after they bolt on different badges or other bits of plastic to signify how 'luxurious', 'prestigious' or 'sporty' a particular model is. (Bizarrely, plastic spoilers and other elements of most 'sports' packages have actually been shown to slow vehicles down.)

Some suppliers of electrical appliances sell identical products under different brands, allowing consumers to decide how much status they would like to have on display in their lounge rooms. Distributors of milk, too, sell identical milk in differently branded bottles at vastly different prices. Factories that produce brand-name shoes one day often churn out cheap shoes the next; literally the only difference is the symbol glued onto the side. If people knew they were sometimes buying products that were actually identical under the logos, it would be a different story.

The purveyors of luxury goods are often in dispute with their Chinese manufacturing plants. The factories often produce much larger quantities of the product than requested, and then sell the surplus as pirated goods at low prices. The only thing that is fake about them is that they do not have permission to attach a particular symbol (a symbol that says 'luxury').

HOW DOES CULTURE CHANGE?

While the term *culture war* is often thrown around in public debate, it is rare to find people who admit to being actively engaged in it. In Western democracies people often believe that culture is innate, and that its evolution (to the extent that it does evolve) is driven by the economy or technology.

Of course the purpose of nearly every advertisement on television is to change our culture. The aim of individual advertisements is to make people feel insecure about something they were once relaxed about – *Do visitors think your bathroom smells? Are your armpits as smooth as your face?* – or to make them attach status to something they were previously unconcerned about – *Did you know that your choice of flooring says a lot about you?*

Over decades, countless advertisements have normalised the idea that we should always be on the lookout for new products to solve new problems. There are no advertisements that remind you that your friends visit you for the pleasure of your company, not for the forest smell in your bathroom; no one would make money from that ad. Similarly, there are no ads reminding you to pay off the debts you have already accumulated before thinking about what else you might buy. Most countries have some form of 'truth in advertising' laws, but such laws only prevent small lies about product attributes. There are no laws to prevent advertisers suggesting that a new car, a new soft drink or a new credit card will make you relaxed, popular or sexy.

Advertising is the most visible and most expensive form of cultural influence in Western countries. Of course, the hundreds of billions of dollars spent telling us how cheap or essential products are must, by definition, drive up the cost of those products. Bizarrely, if the products really were essential, the expensive ads would be a waste of money and we wouldn't need to be encouraged to buy them. Again, it's okay for ads to tell big lies.

But it's not just the ads – the products themselves also shape our culture. Smartphones have transformed the way we communicate, navigate and shop, but they have also transformed our attitude to expensive consumer goods. The high visibility of our mobile phones, compared to our dishwasher or desktop computer, means that their symbolic value is far higher than that of other electronic goods. In turn, the invention and popularity of smartphones is accelerating our cultural willingness to dispose of perfectly functional material goods well before they have ceased to be functional. The fact that so many old mobile phones remain hidden in household cupboards probably reflects the fact that we know phones are too valuable to throw out, but that doesn't stop us from replacing them.

Planned obsolescence – achieved by producing regular 'upgrades' that quickly render a functional product out of date, or by deliberate design that fails quickly and cannot be repaired – also plays a major role in shaping our culture. After decades of products that break easily or don't last, people adapt by lowering their expectations. Similarly, the more that producers offer only short warranties, refuse to manufacture spare parts and make it difficult to open, let alone repair, an expensive device, the easier it is for them to sell you a new model.

Whether firms are punished for producing low-quality goods that don't last long, or rewarded by consumers looking for the latest opportunity to demonstrate how fashionable they are, is entirely a matter of culture. Similarly, cultural choices determine whether scientists and engineers design products that are more durable or harder to repair. If large numbers of middle-class consumers refused to purchase products that were expensive or impossible to repair, or that soon became obsolete, then some profit-seeking companies would respond by trying to give the public what it wanted.

Of course, it is not just advertising and products that shape culture. Politicians, media proprietors, artists, authors, comedians, architects and community groups all do so too. No one doubts that Hitler shaped German culture, and no one doubts that Gandhi shaped Indian, and English, culture. Policy, too, shapes culture. A national decision to provide universal childcare, universal health care or give women the vote reflects a social preference, and the operation of such a policy will likely reshape the culture even further. As I discuss in later chapters, the role of policy in shaping and reshaping culture is easily underestimated.

It's hard to see where culture comes from. Does wearing your grandfather's watch or buying a brand-new one give you higher status? Economists can no more contribute to this question than they can help us decide whether we should buy Coke, Pepsi or no-name cola. But the fact that economists have little to add to our understanding of culture doesn't mean that cultural change does not have significant economic consequences.

The private sector has become expert in selling status at a time when the public sector has largely vacated the terrain. Once upon a time, teaching, nursing and policing were highly admired professions. The pay was never the best, but the community supplemented the modest income with a generous helping of status. But sustained attacks on public education have led to professions such as teaching slipping down the ranks of the most respected professions. A UK survey compared the career goals of school kids in 2009 with those twenty-five years earlier. While the top three professions in 1984 were Teacher, Banker and Medicine, by 2009 they had morphed into Sports Star, Pop Star and Actor/Actress.[1]

WON'T TECHNOLOGY SOLVE OUR PROBLEMS FOR US?

It is pretty strange to think that the solution to the problem of how to dispose of billions of plastic bottles each year – bottles that could carry water for centuries – is to find a way to make them break down faster. It's even stranger to think that the solution to the obesity epidemic is to spend billions of dollars developing weight-loss drugs.

There's no doubt that the profit motive has given rise to the single-use water bottle. And developing the scientific knowhow to make a perfectly clear plastic bottle that is strong enough to store water for years but weak enough not to last for centuries would be impressive. But we must note that the search for such a 'perfect plastic bottle' is underpinned by our cultural wish to use plastic bottles in a very strange way. While science and economics play a supporting role, the key driver is our willingness to spend more per litre on bottled water than we spend on petrol – and then, having done so, to throw away today's bottle and pay for a new one tomorrow.

When we understand the centrality of culture to so much of our economic activity, it becomes clear why the debate about technological change – is it the cause of the world's problems or the solution? – is as heated as it is unhelpful. Like debates about what is 'fair', what is 'sustainable' and whether or not football should be called soccer, there is no meaningful answer to the question of whether technological developments are good or bad. Nuclear medicine has saved many, many lives, but nuclear accidents at Chernobyl and Fukushima have killed thousands of people, devastated the lives of millions, cost billions and will harm the natural environment and human health for millennia. To be clear, no technology is good or bad, although the uses to which it is put can be.

Technology will not determine the fashionable length of skirts next year or the fashionable width of neckties, nor will it decide whether in ten years' time we will still use billions of disposable pens each year, or whether we will aspire to own just one high-quality refillable pen for our entire life. Indeed, technology won't determine whether we need pens at all, or whether our fingertips and screens will replace paper and ink.

Just as a culture of vegetarianism is a far better predictor of a country's demand for beef than the price of meat, the presence of a wasteful culture is a far better predictor of the demand for paper plates than the price of the plates. A growing number of US households now regularly eat dinner from paper plates to avoid the need for washing up. Whether this trend takes off in other countries will be affected more by culture than by regulation or so-called market forces.

The decision to build the Fukushima nuclear power plant near the sea in a region in which earthquakes and tsunamis are common was not the fault of the scientists and engineers who pioneered nuclear science. Nor was the decision to build a large number of nuclear power stations before any long-term sites for the safe storage of nuclear waste. The decision in some countries to let people drive without seatbelts or own automatic guns reflects a cultural view of risk, as do decisions about nuclear power, climate change, air pollution and genetic modification. Science will always create new possibilities for causing harm or rendering help. Culture dictates which choices we make.

Culture determines how much meat we eat. It also determines whether we are likely to eat dog, horse, pig or cow meat. It determines whether we buy our pets special beds or let them sleep on old blankets. It determines whether we are likely to buy alcohol and tobacco, and whether we go out for coffee, make it ourselves or abstain from wicked stimulants. Culture determines whether we are likely to work on Sundays or shop on Sundays, and how likely we are to buy lots of things that our loved ones don't need in late December. Culture drives the shape and the size of our economies, and economists typically assume – as we have seen, with 'all else remaining equal' – that culture is fixed and unchanging. It's not.

IBM executives once believed that the world demand for computers might be in the dozens, not the billions, but they weren't alone in their inability to predict the future. Culture will determine whether it is fashionable to have a big, fast car that you can drive yourself or whether it is more prestigious to be picked up by a small, autonomous electric car that allows you to work and play as you move around your city. Culture will determine whether genetic modification of human embryos is seen as playing God, or as giving your kids their best chance in life. Culture will determine whether working long hours is a sign of status and importance, or evidence of poor time management.

Technology can broaden the range of possible options, and change the relative cost of different products. But culture determines which options are desirable – and once we decide something is desirable, we don't care much about its price. That's why we happily pay so much for bottled water and complain about the price of petrol. Culture shapes the economy, and affluenza has shaped our culture.

BUT DON'T MARKETS DRIVE CHANGE?

The idea that 'market forces', like some sort of gravitational pull, are somehow beyond the influence of mere mortals is as widely held as it is debilitating for those who want to change the world.

Markets don't force us to do anything. Indeed, markets don't want anything, need anything or demand anything. Markets are simply a place where buyers and sellers come together. Whether a market is a physical place, like a fish market, or a virtual space, like eBay or a stock market, it is the motivations, desires and relative power of individual buyers and sellers that shape outcomes, not some external 'force'.

When a plane crashes and hundreds of passengers die, we inevitably inquire into the cause of the accident. You could argue that all plane crashes are caused by the same thing: gravity. But such an explanation would be meaningless. The existence of gravity is taken for granted; what matters is who did what, and when. Did the pilot make an error? Did a maintenance worker make an error? Was a key part of the plane faulty when it left the factory?

When hundreds of people lose their lives, the community demands answers.

But when a financial market collapses and millions of people lose their life savings, you'll often hear people dismissively blame 'market forces'. Doing this is a great way of ensuring that individuals duck responsibility, and of convincing the millions of people who elect democratic governments that some reforms are impossible because 'the market would react angrily'. What that really means is 'rich people who own a lot of shares would react angrily'.

The market didn't open our cities up to cars, communities did. They did so by making it legal to drive cars in cities, by funding the building of sealed roads, by appropriating the land the roads need. And, in many cities, by ripping up the tramlines that provided cheap and convenient competition for cars.

Those who claim that 'you can't stand in the way of the market' are often the same people who claim that we must win 'the war on drugs', and that to legalise the sale of marijuana, for example, would be to give in to drug dealers. They are also often the same people who oppose the legalisation of abortion and the legalisation of prostitution. The line between culture and economics is far blurrier than many in power would like to admit, but for those interested in driving change it is critical to understand the distinction between the two, and how they interact.

MATERIALISM AS A DRIVER OF ECONOMIC CHANGE

If people loved their things, cared for them, maintained and repaired them and then handed them on to others who did likewise, the global economy would be transformed, as would the impact of human activity on the natural environment.

But if people continue to embrace the benefits of 'convenience' and pursue the symbolic appeal of novelty, then, as billions more people emulate the consumption patterns of today's middle-class culture, the impact on the natural environment will be devastating.

It is physically impossible for the production of stuff to grow exponentially for another thousand years. It's probably impossible for it to grow exponentially for another hundred. And if the world is to avoid dangerous climate change, the trajectory of human consumption will need to change radically in the coming decade. It's not complicated. Everyone knows that we need to change direction; the debate is about the timing.

Consider the following. Billions of tonnes of food are thrown away each year because fruit has spots on it, because leafy vegetables show signs of snails, or because producers put misleading 'best before' dates on their packaging. Millions of tonnes of oil are transformed into plastic bottles, which, while lasting for thousands of years, are intended to be used once and then thrown away.

In 2015 American consumers spent over US$14 billion buying over 40 billion litres of bottled water. Bottled water consumption has been growing steadily for the past decade, except in 2008 and 2009, during the global financial crisis. Despite its decline in those years, no deaths through dehydration due to a shortage of bottled water were reported.

The bottled water industry is preparing for continued growth. Indeed, according to the international bottled water association: 'Bottled water's versatility makes it suitable for consumption at any time of day and in just about any setting or situation.'[2] The association also states: 'Consumers' interest in beverages that deliver benefit above and beyond simple refreshment also contributes to the quintessential hydrating beverage's ascension in the beverage rankings.'[3]

Whether consumers around the world choose to double their spending on bottled water in the coming decade or decide to carry their own water will not be determined by the relative cost of bottled water and the cost of a thermos. It will be determined by culture.

Whether people see access to consumer credit as a source of convenience or as a cost to their lifetime spending will be determined by culture.

Whether they see brown spots on a banana as a signal to eat it straightaway or a signal to throw it away will be determined by culture.

And whether buying goods that need to be disposed of each year is seen as a source of status or a source of shame will be determined by culture.

While no one is in charge of culture, there is no doubt that some people, companies and countries put far more effort into shaping it than others.

The following chapters argue that those who want to reduce greenhouse-gas emissions, reduce deforestation or increase the ability of people to spend quality time with their friends, families and communities will need to spend as much time thinking about the cultural drivers of the problems they seek to solve as developing 'policy solutions' to them.

The best cure for environmental problems is prevention. And the best way to prevent human consumption patterns from doing enormous environmental harm is to cure our culture of the disease of affluenza.

Craig Bennett

It's very curious what politicians, the media and the public get excited about, and what they choose not to get quite so excited about.

Take, for example, air pollution. Government scientists estimate that air pollution is contributing to the premature deaths of around 40,000 people in Britain every single year. The total cost to public health is estimated to be around £20 billion, approximately 16 per cent of the annual budget of the National Health Service.

And yet, the response of most British politicians to this crisis has been to do the bare minimum, and even then to dither and delay as much as is bureaucratically possible (which is quite a lot). The UK government has, after all, lost a series of court cases because it is failing to meet basic European Union air quality standards.

Just imagine, for a moment, that it wasn't our petrol and diesel cars, buses and trucks causing 40,000 premature deaths every year, but – oh, I don't know – a Middle Eastern dictator spraying chemical weapons over the population. How would we, the public, respond? How would we expect our politicians to act?

Would we be happy if the government were to publish a plan with the resolute aim of resolving the problem more than twenty years hence? No, we most certainly would not. We would expect an immediate end to the threat, within days, and wouldn't tolerate government focus on anything else until it had been dealt with.

How would newspapers respond to proposals to consider only 'targeted' measures in some of the most heavily affected areas? They would call for the government to be ousted and for Churchill to be brought back from the grave.

The deadly problem with air pollution is that, first, we've all become used to it, and second, it's caused by our own actions.

For these simple, arbitrary reasons, we place much less importance on ending it than if it were being inflicted on us by a hostile foreign power.

And yet, the very fact that it is caused by our own actions means the solutions are so much easier to deliver, and come with a much higher probability of success than, for example, military action aimed at stopping an aggressor. We could solve the scandal of air pollution very quickly, if we wanted to. But in most cities, most of the time, we choose not to.

Craig Bennett is the CEO of Friends of the Earth (England, Wales and Northern Ireland) and honorary professor of Sustainability and Innovation at the Alliance Manchester Business School.

3.

Lighten Up

'A love of nature keeps no factories busy.'

Aldous Huxley, *Brave New World*

Activity is not evidence of achievement. Being busy is not proof of productivity. Throwing away unused things is the very opposite of efficient. And increasing the amount of stuff that is bought and sold is not in itself a sign of a strong economy. In fact, when much of the stuff being produced is of no real use, and when much of it was purchased with borrowed money, such economic activity is more likely to weaken an economy than strengthen it.

The stated goal of economics is the efficient allocation of scarce resources. But as we have seen, consumerism results in countless tonnes of perfectly useable food, appliances, clothes and sporting equipment being thrown away each year. While some of the raw materials might be recycled, the labour and energy that went into producing products that have hardly been used is lost forever. Likewise, the enormous amount of labour and energy used to transport these things to and from factories, warehouses, shops, households and garbage dumps is lost forever. The only legacy of these products is the harm that was done to the natural environment in order to enable their brief and often useless lifespan.

In recent times, the conventional wisdom in most Western countries has been that private-sector activity is inherently efficient, and that while some public-sector activity is a necessary evil, a large public sector is evidence of inefficiency and the need for 'reform'. By this logic, if the time, effort and resources wasted producing unwanted foot spas were redirected to the provision of public health or education, it would be evidence of a growing inefficiency. Conversely, the less a country spends on public health and public education, the more efficient it supposedly is. Indeed, the process of making things people don't need and then recycling them into other things they don't need is called now called 'wealth creation' or 'job creation'. More accurate descriptions would be 'resource destruction' and 'waste creation'.

In his book *The General Theory of Employment, Interest and Money*, the economist John Maynard Keynes once posed the following thought experiment:

> If the Treasury were to fill old bottles with banknotes, bury them at suitable depths in disused coalmines which are then filled up to the surface with town rubbish, and leave it to private enterprise on well-tried

principles of laissez-faire to dig the notes up again ...
there need be no more unemployment and, with
the help of the repercussions, the real income of the
community, and its capital wealth also, would probably
become a good deal greater than it actually is. It would,
indeed, be more sensible to build houses and the like;
but if there are political and practical difficulties in the
way of this, the above would be better than nothing.

Keynes was making the important (and, at the time,
radical) point that if the government wanted to create jobs,
it could simply fund the construction of useful infrastructure, or even useless hole-digging. But many of his modern
counterparts seem to have taken him literally about the
garbage while ignoring his point about the public sector.
Today, factories create a torrent of wasted resources, from
which recyclers extract some remnant with which the factories can repeat the process. And the faster they do it, the
more 'economic activity' they create, and the richer we are
told our countries are becoming.

There is no doubt that the cycle of production, consumption, disposal, recycling and production creates
economic activity, jobs and, for some in the supply chain,
wealth. But does this process in any way ensure the efficient
allocation of scarce resources? Is throwing away functional
goods really a good way to 'make the economy strong'?

WHY DON'T ECONOMISTS CARE ABOUT WASTE?

'You can mine for gold, but you can sell pickaxes.'

Anonymous

One of the biggest fortunes made in the Californian gold rush of the nineteenth century was that of Levi Strauss, who made his money selling everything from tents and buckets to the denim pants that still bear his name. He got paid whether his customers found gold or not. All retailers make money whether we find happiness in the products they sell us or not. Indeed, the longer people search for gold, or happiness, the more pants and other stuff Mr Strauss and other retailers can sell them.

Affluenza has fuelled a massively inefficient search for happiness. Rather than dig through the earth in search of gold, or dig through Keynes' rubbish dump looking for bottles of money, modern capitalism relies on billions of people searching for new products that will fill the hole in their lives that was briefly plugged by the last purchase. The banks, the manufacturers, the advertisers and the retailers all make their fortune by selling us the dream that 'there's happiness in them there hills'. Of course, the last thing retailers want is for us actually to find it.

As we have seen, poorly understood economic indicators such as GDP help to ensure the global debate about building strong economies focuses on the flawed idea that the amount of economic activity is in some way a proxy for the rate of economic or social progress. In fact, the empirical link between growth in the size of an economy and human happiness is very weak – some would say non-existent. This should come as no surprise. Consider the following:

- No shareholder would be impressed to learn that their company was spending lots of time and money having meetings with itself, even if the meetings required a lot of expensive travel that necessitated new teams of people dedicated to booking that travel.

- No parent would be impressed to find that their child had spent hours moving the mess from one side of their bedroom to the other.

- No government would be pleased to have riots and vandalism, even if they caused a boom in the local window repair, painting and construction industries.

So why are politicians and business leaders impressed when told that GDP has grown because of a spike in the consumption of imported appliances and bottled water (otherwise known as 'strong retail sales figures')?

The answer is both simple and cynical. Wasting natural resources to produce stuff that will soon be thrown away doesn't generate true national wealth, but it does generate enormous wealth for some people in the supply chain. That's all it does, and that wealth creation is naturally very,

very important to those people. But to suggest that borrowing money from overseas to buy things that were made overseas – things that are quickly thrown out and buried in local landfill – plays an important role in making a national economy strong is simply absurd.

It is hard to believe that all the rowing machines that accumulate in the spare rooms of the nation might be seen as an indicator of wealth or progress. But, as enormous amounts of energy, natural resources and human labour are wasted on making products that are never used, or that are designed to fall apart, what have the economists and politicians had to say about this consumerism-induced waste? Almost nothing, except for implicit praise. Indeed, rather than highlight the economic and environmental harm of such waste, an enormous number of economists and politicians have spent decades trying to shift the rules of global trade, and the norms of 'sensible economic policy', to generate more such waste.

The term 'Washington Consensus' has often been used to summarise the fundamental tenets of the neoliberal agenda at the global level. According to its adherents, who have shrunk in visibility if not number since Donald Trump was elected and the UK supported Brexit, the way to increase the efficiency of an economy is:

- To cut tax rates for wealthy citizens, allowing them to spend more money on consumer goods;

- To cut taxes on businesses, allowing them to appropriate a larger share of national income, on the promise that they will invest some of the proceeds into the production of more stuff;

- To cut spending on the labour-intensive community services used most heavily by low-income earners (such as public schools, hospitals and public transport), on the basis that such activity is inefficient and crowds out more efficient private-sector activity;

- To cut the wages of low-income earners, who spend the smallest proportion of their income on the disposable consumer goods that have the highest profit margins;

- To reduce protections for workers, consumers and the environment, so as to increase producer profits; and

- To increase trade with developing countries whose environmental, labour and consumer protections are much lower to help reduce such standards in developed countries.

While there is no doubt that there are times when lowering trade barriers can lead to an increase in the quality of life of some people in some countries, there is also no doubt that far more effort has been expended by groups such as the World Bank and the International Monetary Fund on trying to reduce trade barriers than on trying to reduce water pollution and income inequality – which have also been shown to improve economic performance and human wellbeing.

Once we draw a distinction between whether an activity will create wealth for a producer and whether it will create wellbeing for a community, it becomes much easier to decode the flood of econobabble used to justify the obsession among advocates of the Washington Consensus for lower taxes and less regulation rather than for reduced tax evasion and more environmental regulation. While it is possible for the owners of multinational companies to profit from poor labour and environmental standards in low-income countries that export stuff to rich countries, it is far harder for rich people in rich countries to benefit from an improvement in the standard of living of workers in those developing countries.

Economists have always been aware of the difference between the amount of stuff a nation consumes and the wellbeing of its citizens. The question we must ask is not 'Why don't the economists get it?' but 'Why don't the economists say much about it?'

A cynical answer to that question is that most economists operate on the assumption that the customer is always right. So when the IMF and the World Bank offer to pay economists to explain the benefits of using borrowed money to buy new stuff, most of them are happy to take the money. On the other hand, many economists have highlighted the problems with placing the pursuit of GDP ahead of the pursuit of community wellbeing, but such economists are far less likely to be asked to give keynote addresses at the most 'prestigious' events. Culture shapes not just economics, but the economists anointed to explain economics to the populace.

ALL ECONOMIC ACTIVITY WAS NOT CREATED POLITICALLY EQUAL

If millions of people voluntarily gave up buying bottled water tomorrow and instead donated the money they saved to medical research, there would be no reduction in GDP, but there would be a devastating impact on those who profit from the sale of bottled water. There would also be a surge of new jobs in medical research. Given how few people are employed to fill a bottle with water and how labour-intensive research is, there would likely even be an increase in overall employment.

Similarly, if a tax was imposed on the sugary drinks that cause so much ill health, and the tax revenue used to fund a labour-intensive program such as active playgroups for kids, supporters of small government would likely scream about the inefficiency of a program that improved health and created jobs at no net cost to the budget.

It's not the size of government that is a key concern for many conservatives, but the size of the private sector's profit margin. When we spend $100 on pie makers and table-top electric wine chillers, the majority of the money goes as profit to the owners of the various parts of the supply chain, but when we spend $100 on a publicly funded teacher, nurse or aged-care worker, there is little or no profit margin to be sliced off. That's why the proponents of small government who rage against excessive spending on public health care usually don't mind huge public expenditure on aircraft carriers and fighter jets. They know the military hardware will be built by the private sector and that the manufacturers, like Levi Strauss, will make their profits whether or not the ships, jets and weapons are ever used. The shape of our economy doesn't just determine how much harm is done to the environment, it helps determine how much profit will be collected by the owners of the supply chain. One thing that manufacturers, retailers, advertisers and transport companies can agree on is that none of them make a buck out of higher taxes being used to fund better quality high schools.

While choosing which activities do most to improve community wellbeing will always be controversial, identifying the economic consequences of such choices is quite straightforward. For example, if consumers shifted away from buying lots of stuff towards buying lots of services, it would have a huge impact on the *shape* of the economy but almost no impact on its *size*. And if citizens switched their spending away from stuff they didn't need and towards services that governments provide efficiently – health care, education, public transport, bigger parks and more museums – there would be no reduction in the size of GDP, but there would be a significant reduction in the amount of profit earned in the economy (the profit margin on $1000 worth of publicly provided childcare is a lot smaller than the profit margin on $1000 worth of branded merchandise . . . but there are more jobs created per dollar spent on childcare than for each dollar spent on handbags and sunglasses).

A shift away from privately provided stuff towards publicly provided services would also lead to much lower consumption of natural resources. Yet as long as people get the same or more satisfaction from high-quality public services as they do from foot spas they don't use and food they throw away, this shift would have no adverse impact on the happiness of citizens. Indeed, people would likely be happier.

THE TIMES HAVE ALWAYS BEEN A-CHANGIN'

Once upon a time, enormous quantities of copper wire were required to connect every household to every other household to enable phone calls; over time, much of this copper was replaced by fibre-optic cable. But a growing number of households, and even entire countries, are now relying heavily (in some cases entirely) on wireless transmission of information. The composition of economic activity is always shifting in response to technological change, social change and change in the relative price of things. In turn, the impact on the natural environment and the distribution of jobs, income and political power is also ever-changing. The way we make phone calls is just one example of this.

Through the second half of the twentieth century, telephone handsets sat unchanging in households around the world. But while few people in those days thought to 'update' their home phone, these days we replace our smartphones every couple of years. The batteries in the hundreds of millions of smartphones we now rely on have driven global demand for rare earth minerals to record levels; in turn, extraction of these minerals has surged. Hundreds of thousands of telephone operators have lost their jobs in recent decades, but hundreds of thousands of mobile phone salespeople, technicians and screen repairers have been employed. But while mobile phone technology is improving steadily, the main reason for rapidly replacing smartphones is cultural, not functional. Like a new car and some new shoes, for many people (not you, of course, dear reader, but others) the main function of a new phone is symbolic, not material. New phones make us cool.

It is not just the wealth, political influence and environmental impact of the phone companies that are affected by the changing technological and cultural drivers of phone choice. Those who own and work in the copper mines are highly unlikely to own and work in the rare earth mines.

Even if the old telephone operators and the newly employed mobile phone salespeople are all members of a union, it is unlikely they are members of the same union. And even though the extraction of copper and the extraction of rare earths both harm the natural environment, it is unlikely that the same rivers, the same farmers and the same species will be harmed.

Changing what we buy destroys jobs, industries, the political power of some groups and different parts of the environment. But we do it all the time. Few politicians stood up for the workers in photo development labs (remember them?) when digital cameras became popular. But many politicians proudly stand up for coal workers threatened by the growing preference for renewable energy. A simple explanation might that the profits and political power of the coal industry are bigger and more focused than those of the small-business people who owned the photo development labs.

The fact that the composition of the things we produce and consume will inevitably change over time is cold comfort to those people harmed by change. Indeed, the fact that moving from film cameras to phone cameras might reduce the cost of living, reduce the impact of photography on the environment and drive the creation of new companies such as Instagram does not mean that Kodak or its workers were excited about the increase in economic efficiency associated with that technological change.

The following sections provide a wide range of examples of how cultural and technological change can reshape the economy in ways that will reduce environmental harm. But as the oil, gas and coal industries' response to climate change shows, those who have hundreds of billions of dollars invested in a specific product have hundreds of billions of reasons to focus on influencing the technological, cultural and policy context in which that product is sold.

Put simply, the potential for future benefits for the broader community will do nothing to reduce the determination of those who profit from the status quo to oppose change. As Renaissance political thinker Niccolò Machiavelli observed:

> There is nothing more difficult to take in hand, more perilous to conduct, or more uncertain in its success, than to take the lead in the introduction of a new order of things. For the reformer has enemies in all those who profit by the old order, and only lukewarm defenders in all those who would profit by the new order, this lukewarmness arising partly from fear of their adversaries ... and partly from the incredulity of mankind, who do not truly believe in anything new until they have had actual experience of it.

RICH ECONOMIES ARE GETTING LIGHTER

People in Western countries are consuming less steel, less oil, less electricity, less paper and a lot less photographic film than they once did. While some of this is explained by the shift of manufacturing to developing countries, the change is mainly driven by culture and technology.

Car ownership has always been much lower in New York than in Los Angeles, but it is declining steadily among young people in developed countries around the world. In the US the proportion of 20- to 24-year-olds with a driver's licence fell from 91.8 per cent to 76.7 per cent between 1983 and 2014.[4] In New South Wales, the largest state in Australia, the share of people under twenty-five with a driver's licence has been falling by around 1 per cent per year for the last decade.[5]

Cars, once a symbol of freedom and adulthood for many young people, now call to mind only traffic. (Also relevant, perhaps, is the fact that cars render young drivers unable to interact with their friends on social media as they move around the city. Technology influences culture.) Significantly for those who think 'price signals' such as a carbon tax hold the answers to all environmental problems, both cars and oil are becoming cheaper. It's not price that is changing the transport choices of young people.

A major determinant of the demand for steel, concrete, oil and insurance over the coming century will be the extent to which the cities being built in Africa and Asia pursue the transport and urban design culture of LA, New York, Singapore or Amsterdam. The demand for cars, and in turn the demand for steel and concrete, is significantly shaped by those who choose to promote roads, rails or footpaths in their city's design. The ability to walk to work reduces the amount of economic activity, but there are few (perhaps only those in the car industry) who would consider that a problem, or a sign of a weak economy.

People in the 1980s used to buy a lot of Liquid Paper to correct the mistakes they made with their typewriters. Carbon paper was big too. Carbon paper massively increased the productivity of typists, who could suddenly make two, three or even four copies of a document at once. If they got to the post office early enough each afternoon, documents might even be delivered to recipients the next day. Imagine that!

It's hard, perhaps impossible, for humans to anticipate how technological or cultural change will yield the potential to lighten our material impact on the planet while simultaneously reducing our cost of living and improving our lifestyle. While some saw early on how personal computers might eventually lead to the paperless office (maybe one day it will), few in the 1980s anticipated that smartphones linked to a global internet and a network of GPS satellites would destroy the need for telephone books, printed business directories and street directories. When was the last time you used a fax machine, let alone changed the roll?

(People over the age of about forty will know what I'm talking about.) The savings in time, money and trees associated with the substitution of pixels for paper is enormous.

And it's not just steel and paper. The world's most famous manufacturer of stylish but disposable furniture, IKEA, has suggested that in Western countries we might be approaching 'peak candleholder' and, indeed, peak stuff. In 2016 IKEA's chief sustainability officer said that 'broadly, you saw a tremendous expansion in consumption and people's livelihoods through the twentieth century. And the use of stuff is plateauing out.'[6]

The idea that the amount of stuff we produce will always grow is so hard-wired into modern economic and political debate that questioning the composition of that growth, the ratio of stuff to services, or the idea that people might want to buy more leisure and fewer things, has become anathema. While it is acceptable to discuss the economic effect of a shift from bricks-and-mortar bookstores to online bookstores, it is apparently beyond the scope of polite debate to discuss that middle-class people in rich countries have thrown away so many perfectly functional television sets that many charities will no longer accept old-fashioned cathode-ray TVs – the old ones in a box with a curved screen – because they can't even give them away.

While no economic textbooks, and few politicians, ever actually come out and say it, it is widely accepted that responsible citizens aspire to work more hours and spend more money to keep the economy strong. And if we have to throw away perfectly functional things to make room for them, so be it. A collectivist spirit might be noble, but the idea that we all owe it to the economy to waste time, money and resources is entirely incompatible with the neoliberal tenet of rugged individualists acting solely in their self-interest.

Going one step further, imagine if cultural change led people to make their own coffee and drink it in their own homes. The impact on employment in cafes and on the size of measured GDP of such a simple cultural shift would have a bigger impact on employment in Australia or United States than the immediate closure of all coalmines. Likewise, if billions of people opted for tap water, made their own sandwiches or gave homemade cakes ... Such outbreaks of choice or efficiency would be as devastating for cafes, beverage companies and retailers as digital cameras were for Kodak – but the overall macroeconomic impact would be trivial. The money not spent on coffee would be spent on something else.

People often tend to underestimate the degree to which one good or service can substitute for another – especially in a consumer society, where people spend a lot of money on things that are primarily designed to say something about them. But if one of the main reasons, if not the main reason, to spend $100,000 on a car is for people to say something about themselves, why don't they just buy an ordinary car and pay a famous painter to give it a unique, and expensive, paint job? Of course, while spending $100,000 on a 'sports car' that can't fit your family but can go four times the legal speed limit is an acceptable way to say something about yourself, only a weirdo would support the arts.

The following sections outline simple ways to reshape the economy to significantly reduce the harm done to the natural environment. They are not predictions, but possibilities. The biggest obstacle to realising them will be the harm they could do to the powerful groups profiting from the current mix of goods and services that we take for granted.

EXPERIENCES AS A SUBSTITUTE FOR STUFF

Would you prefer a massage or some new shirts for Christmas? Would you prefer to drive a race car around a track at high speed once a month, or drive a sports car through a traffic jam every weekday morning? Would you prefer to have a world-class chef prepare a meal for you and your guests in your own kitchen, or would you prefer to own a $20,000 oven?

There is, of course, no right answer to these questions. The point is simply that many services can substitute for many goods. Technological and cultural change can help tip the balance towards services, and policy change can amplify or dampen the size of the effect. But the financial, employment and environmental implications of renting a chef rather than buying a new oven are significant.

Probably as a result of countless late-night advertisements, garages around the Western world show proof of the inability of most people to predict their own level of motivation, determination or interest in losing weight, building muscle or having 'killer abs'. Billions of dollars' worth of treadmills, rowing machines and exercise bikes are being used to dry clothes and keep boxes off the ground because millions of people thought that their inactivity was the result of lack of equipment rather than a lack of motivation. Substituting $1000 worth of personal training for $1000 worth of imported machinery would be far more likely to solve the underlying motivational issue, and at the same time help people realise that their local park and the stuff they already have is everything they need to make their bodies stronger and healthier.

Similarly, paying money to learn to sing or dance, to learn a language or even to learn the trapeze will bring at least the same benefit for the economy and for your wellbeing as paying to 'modernise' your lounge-room furniture or kitchen benchtop again.

Finally, although I have significant doubts about the social environment that encourages such choices, it is clear that the growing demand for cosmetic surgery reflects a shift in consumer preference away from stuff and towards services. Regular renovations of the face consume far less of the world's natural resources than regular renovations of the kitchen. That said, a smile might achieve the same result at even lower financial and environmental cost.

LEISURE AS A SUBSTITUTE FOR STUFF

Would you prefer a 4 per cent pay rise or an extra two weeks of paid annual holidays? While surveys suggest that most full-time workers would prefer more time to more money, both the workplace and national culture make the pursuit of more leisure a difficult goal for many workers to pursue. For cultural reasons, putting in long hours and having short holidays is often seen as a signal – to colleagues, family and the community – of one's commitment as a worker. While data suggests that grinding work hours are usually associated with a loss of motivation, camaraderie and productivity, symbolism matters in the workplace as well as the shopping centre.

The problem for individuals who would prefer an extra few weeks at the beach to some extra takeaway food through the year is that, when it comes to signalling one's commitment to a job, it is not the *absolute* number of holidays an individual takes that matters, but the *relative* amount. That is, it's not how many days' leave you take each year that will likely cause you grief, but whether you have more days away than everyone else in your workplace.

In the United States, employers don't have to give workers any paid vacation but typically full-time workers get two weeks. In Canada workers get at least two weeks, and in Australia it's four weeks. European Union countries have a minimum of four weeks, but some, such as France and Germany, have six weeks a year. Imagine that – a month and a half off work each year, on full pay!

Of course, leisure is not just about how many weeks' holidays we have each year. Many people around the world work seven days a week, either from financial necessity or love of their work. The two-day 'weekend' is a historically recent phenomenon, with the term first appearing in print in a British magazine in 1879. Henry Ford starting shutting his factories down for all of Saturday and Sunday in 1926, and the Amalgamated Clothing Workers was the first US union to demand and obtain a two-day weekend in 1929.

The only thing preventing widespread adoption of three-day weekends is culture. That and the adverse impact working less would have on those who make profits from selling us stuff.

Certain employers offer more radical substitutions of time for money. Some teachers in Australia can work full-time for 80 per cent of their normal wage in exchange for working only four years in every five. Every five years they get a whole year off work, on what they have come to know as 'full pay', and they have a secure job to return to. And every five teachers who make such a choice creates a job for a new full-time colleague. It gets better. In most countries there are taxation benefits that accompany such 'smoothing' of income, as the tax payable on four years of full pay and one year of no pay will almost always be more than the tax payable on five years of 80 per cent pay. Who'd have thought taking a year off could be a tax-minimisation and job-creation strategy?

Consider the following:

- If a worker took an extra two weeks' holiday each year instead of a 4 per cent pay rise, their employer might employ a casual worker to perform the extra work. The impact on total wages paid would be approximately zero, but wages would be more evenly distributed across the workforce.

- If a worker took an extra two weeks' holiday each year instead of a 4 per cent pay rise, their employer might decide the business can make do without replacing the worker by spreading tasks over existing workers. In this case, the wage/profit share of national income would change slightly, but the impact on the size of national income would be approximately zero.

- If all workers decided, as they did over the first seventy years of the twentieth century, to gradually and collectively seek to reduce the number of hours they worked each day (the eight-hour-day campaigns), the number of days worked each week (the two-day weekend) and the number of days worked each year (annual leave and public holidays), then the rate of growth in national income would be slower than if the hours worked per year had remained stable. But if such choices were voluntary, and those who wanted to work longer hours were free to do so, then while measured economic activity would be lower, national wellbeing would unarguably be higher.

In 1930 Keynes wrote an essay entitled 'Economic Possibilities for Our Grandchildren', in which he predicted that, by our time, people in rich countries would be working around fifteen hours per week. Needless to say, he was way off, but it was his assumptions about culture, not his economics, that led him astray.

Keynes assumed that as income rose, people would buy more of the things they valued most – and he wrongly assumed that people would value leisure time. Put simply, as new technologies enabled us to produce the same amount of stuff with fewer hours of labour, Keynes thought people would opt for more time off; it is now obvious that, collectively, we have instead opted to have far more stuff than Keynes could ever have imagined, and less leisure than people enjoyed forty years ago. Since governments abandoned the use of Keynesian economic policies to achieve full employment in the 1970s, the average number of hours worked by full-time employees has increased significantly in most developed countries.

While all rich countries spent the first three-quarters of the twentieth century converting technological progress and productivity growth into shorter working hours, not all rich countries have reversed course as fast as the United States and Australia. France, for example, enshrined the 35-hour working week in law. Northern European countries have pursued significant increases in paid holidays, with weekend work now less common in Europe than in the USA. Of course, no culture is permanent. In the 1950s and 1960s, as Europe rebuilt after the destruction of World War II, the average European worked more hours each year than the average US citizen. The Americans might have won the war, but they lost their leisure time.

While we'll consider the obstacles to shorter working hours in subsequent chapters, the idea that middle- and high-income earners in rich countries could consume more leisure time instead of more stuff has enormous potential to improve the quality of their lives, health and relationships. To give a sense of scale, if the richest 10 per cent of US citizens decided to buy an extra two weeks' annual leave (and lowered their wages by 4 per cent), they would have $80 billion less to spend. That's a lot more leisure time and a lot less stuff to dust and dispose of.

There's something else, too. The more people take weekends and holidays, the more fun it is for other people to take weekends and holidays. Put simply, the benefit an individual gets from taking time off increases when their friends or family take time off as well. (That is, if they like their friends and family ...)

SHARING INSTEAD OF BUYING

While we try hard to teach our children to share, most adult consumers in rich countries avoid the practice themselves. While we might lend our ladder to a neighbour, it's a rare pair of neighbours who will go halves in a lawnmower. Why would anyone want to save half the price of a lawnmower when to do so would limit your ability to use it any time you want?

Whether sharing is informal (between friends and family), formalised (through wider community networks) or commercialised (with people hiring rather than owning seldom-used appliances), it has great potential to make better use of scarce resources, reduce the cost of living and reduce pressure on the environment.

While the financial and environmental benefits of households owning only a share of a lawnmower, a leaf blower, a chainsaw, a bench saw and a demolition drill are substantial, so too are the personal and financial benefits of discussing the use of these tools with others in the community. Many people have the time and motivation, but not the confidence, to take on small repair jobs around the house. And many others enjoy sharing their knowledge and experience with those who want to learn something new. Sharing is an opportunity to save money and natural resources, but it's also a great way to make friends.

REPAIRING AND RESELLING INSTEAD OF BUYING

While most car owners and homeowners are willing to spend significant amounts of money to maintain and repair their cars and homes, few people seek to get their television repaired. It wasn't always this way.

We've already discussed how manufacturers today often engineer 'designed obsolescence' in their products, but they also build them in ways that make repair impossible or impractical. While product replacement might be more profitable for producers than product repair, the net effect is that costs for consumers rise. Similarly, as repair is more time-intensive than mass production, and requires more skill, it is likely that a community that repairs goods would employ more people, per dollar spent, than a community that instinctively disposes of them. Put simply, a shift back to a 'repair culture' could reduce the cost of living, save natural resources and create high-skill jobs. The only thing scary about such a scenario is the potential impact on some companies' profits.

But as we have seen, the cultural desire to purchase new products for symbolic rather than material reasons is, in part, the responsibility of consumers. The re-emergence of a significant repair industry would likely require simultaneous shifts in consumer culture, production processes and regulation.

There are hopeful signs. The emergence of 3D printing is likely to give significant impetus to a repair culture, as 3D printers allow for the timely and low-cost production of the tiny bits of plastic and metal which a repair often requires. As manufacturers have no incentive to encourage repair, they often put little, if any, effort into distribution of spare parts. Indeed, it has been estimated that the cost of buying the spare parts required to build an entire car is more than five times the cost of a new car – and that's before you include the labour required to assemble it.[7] The ability of households, communities or repair technicians to produce their own spare parts has the potential to overcome manufacturers' evident lack of enthusiasm for spare parts. *Forbes* magazine has reported that 3D printing is already a real threat to the $400 billion spare-parts industry.[8]

LOOKS CAN KILL

While our cultural norms and aesthetic preferences are often arbitrary, their consequences can be quite deadly. A preference for ivory carvings, a taste for shark fin or a man's hope that eating ground-up tiger penis might make him virile can have devastating impacts on wild animal populations and even lead to the extinction of entire species. The way we like to look, like our houses to look and like our communities to look drives enormous amounts of economic activity and, often, enormous amounts of need-less environmental harm.

The largest irrigated crop in the United States is the household lawn. The historian Virginia Scott Jenkins observed that the cultural shift towards irrigated, fertilised and weed-free 'lawn' took place after World War II. She argues that 'American front lawns are a symbol of man's control of, or superiority over, his environment'.[9] While the perfect lawn is not pursued quite as vigorously in most other countries, it is not unheard of. Many Australians and Canadians take their mowing and weeding very seriously, but the average townhouse or country house in England is less likely to have a manicured lawn.

The pursuit of a pristine patch of grass makes no more or less sense symbolically than a preference for ironed clothes, shiny hair or bathrooms that smell like an indus-trial chemist thinks flowers should smell. The pursuit of (or rejection of) symbols plays an important role in all communities, and, as discussed in Chapter 2, those who wish to change the world need to take the role of symbols as seriously as they take 'evidence-based policy' or a cost/benefit analysis. In turn, rather than assert that it is 'the economy' that is doing enormous harm to the environ-ment, it would be more accurate to say that 'the culture' is.

For example, imagine if the growing of vegetables at home or the production of homemade vegetable oil was seen as a symbol of humanity's control over our environment, rather than the cultivation of a species of grass that can only survive in an urban environment when provided with enormous quantities of water, fertiliser and pesticide.[10] Imagine if the billions of gallons of water used each day to water American lawns and the millions of tonnes of fertiliser poured onto those lawns each year were, instead, dedicated to the production of nutritious vegetables, which could then be consumed by the household that grew them, or exchanged with neighbours who have chosen to grow different crops.

Such cultural and aesthetic preferences are neither new nor uncommon – they simply shrank in popularity after World War II, when the massive boost in the productivity of Western economies, driven by the war-time need to produce weapons, was redirected to the provision of modern consumer goods.

During World War II, governments reshaped their societies to increase their productive capacity. In Australia, Prime Minister John Curtin launched a propaganda campaign encouraging Australians to 'Dig for Victory' and grow their own vegetables to support the war effort. Garden armies were formed, 'victory gardens' were created, and local governments prompted and incentivised participation by, among other things, awarding volunteers a badge with a 'three carrot' design.

Victory gardens were common in many countries during both world wars, with the term used in Australia,

Canada, the United Kingdom and the United States. By 1943 there were 12 million household victory gardens in the US, and these accounted for one-third of all vegetable production. Tellingly, the US Department of Agriculture was initially opposed to Eleanor Roosevelt planting such a garden in the grounds of the White House, for fear that the movement would harm the nation's agriculture industry.

Would a shift from growing lawns to growing vegetables represent 'an increase in the efficiency of the economy', or would it be 'harmful' and 'cost jobs'?

GETTING EQUAL

The whole point of conspicuous consumption is to try to signal relative wealth, status and prestige, which means that if everyone in society had identical amounts of wealth and status, then such displays would be entirely ineffective. What would be the point in buying a new car every two years to impress your neighbours if all of your neighbours earned exactly the same as you? Indeed, under such circumstances, your neighbours might interpret your decision to update your car as evidence that you were planning to have a cheap holiday or postponing getting your roof fixed.

The greater the disparity in incomes in a society, and the greater the acceptance of the desirability of that disparity, the greater the opportunities for conspicuous consumption will be. When the gap between rich and poor is as enormous as the gradations between middle class, comfortable, affluent, rich and loaded are numerous, then the signalling significance of watches, handbags and sunglasses is very high, as is the likelihood of an outbreak of affluenza.

But it is not just disparities in relative income that can drive our consumption patterns. On average, rich people waste more money than poor people, they buy more food they don't eat, they buy more clothes they don't wear and they even buy more house, or even houses, than they can really use.[11] The transfer through tax reform of billions of dollars from those who don't know what to do with their money to those who have to borrow to make ends meet would, therefore, mean that society consumes less disposable stuff.

A society in which income is more evenly distributed than it is in ours would need far less concrete overall to build its homes (there would be fewer holiday homes, for example), less timber and plastic to furnish them, and less electricity to heat and cool them. In Australia, the average size of a new house has more than doubled in sixty years, from about 100 square metres in 1950 to about 230 square metres today.[12] Meanwhile the average household has fallen from 3.7 people to 2.6.[13] In other words, Australians have gone from 27 square metres per person to 88 square metres per person. Australia is not the only country to see this trend. In the USA, new single-family houses have gone from 154 square metres in 1973 to 222 square metres in 2010.[14] Household size went from 3.0 to 2.6 people.[15]

The indirect impacts of a more equal society are likely to be even more important. In a society where there is a significant gap between those with the most and those with the least, and a culture that attaches significant honour to being wealthy and significant shame to being poor, the amount of money we spend on social signalling is substantial. Imagine if we spent our excess money on something more worthwhile, or at least less destructive.

INFORMATION AS A SUBSTITUTE FOR CARS AND CONCRETE

It would have been hard, if not impossible, to imagine in 1980 that 'data' stored 'in the cloud' would one day be a substitute for photographic film, printed photographs and photo albums. Similarly, in the 1970s the idea that information would be a substitute for the materials dedicated to the storage of music on vinyl and cassette tapes would have seemed far-fetched. Today, the idea that information could be a substitute for the bricks and mortar in our homes (and holiday homes), and the metal in our cars (and taxis) seems equally unlikely. But it is already happening.

Around the world, Uber, Airbnb and their many rivals are already reducing the ratio of cars to passengers, and hotel rooms to tourists. Just as neighbourhood sharing can reduce the number of lawnmowers and bench saws a street needs, technology and culture are already significantly reducing the amount of material resources a community requires to meet its transport and accommodation needs. For many travellers, unused cars, spare bedrooms and empty holiday houses are now attractive substitutes for private car ownership or hotel rooms.

Working from home, similarly, has enormous potential to reduce an economy's ratio of concrete to GDP. Just as the average car is in use 5 per cent of the time, most office workers require two (sometimes three) physical spaces to meet their needs: a home, an office and (for some) a holiday home. A person who is in their office is not in their home. Many jobs, of course, require the physical presence of an employee in a traditional workplace – a waiter, a cleaner, the police – but there is also no doubt that culture, rather than necessity, is a major determinant of the amount of time people spend at a workplace.

Technological and cultural changes create opportunities for office work to be relocated from expensive and materials-intensive office buildings, which of course are largely empty for more than half the time. Enormous amounts of space are currently dedicated to the display of new cars, because of the cultural norm that someone seeking to inspect or test-drive a car should travel to the seller's car yard. Tesla has shown that it is not only possible but actually profitable for a car dealer to bring the car to you. Intriguingly, just as laws about flag-bearers initially slowed the transition to car use, laws prevent Tesla selling cars in some US states as it lacks a traditional dealer network.

Speaking of cars: for every billion commuters who work from home just one day per week, there are roughly 100 billion fewer commuting trips per year (two trips per week, around fifty times per year). That is a lot less demand for petrol, cars, roads and concrete. And even if those billion people still chose to own their own cars, their reduced use frees up an enormous supply of peak-hour vehicles for others to take advantage of via ride-sharing services such as Uber.

MATERIALS AS A SUBSTITUTE FOR MATERIALS

The houses of families with children are often full of plastic toys, which, while once cherished, end up waiting to be chucked away. Much of this plastic will be buried as landfill. Some of it will be recycled, but the energy costs from transporting huge volumes of plastic from family homes to recycling plants, to toy factories, to warehouses, to retail outlets and back to family homes (in elaborate new and disposable packaging) is far from trivial.

Imagine if, when children tired of them, toys could be melted down and converted by a 3D printer into new plastic toys for the same household. Even more efficient would be for communities to share a 3D printing facility. Not only do such 3D printers exist, some can even fabricate consumer products from metal. In fact, some 3D printers have the capacity to make 3D printers!

Of course, it's not just children's toys that clutter up our houses. Most kitchens have a drawer full of plastic and metal devices that haven't been used for years, and most garages have a stockpile of unwanted things. Over the last fifty years the idea has emerged that toys, utensils and even appliances are disposable – but this notion is not irreversible. The financial and environmental benefits of households and communities themselves reusing raw materials are enormous. Such a change would also encourage and reward creativity.

IS THE CONSUMER KING OR ARE WE ALL JUST VICTIMS?

Do factories make the products we demand, or do we demand the products that factories make? Economists assume that the consumer is king and that manufacturers respond to our preferences, yet Steve Jobs and Elon Musk have argued that consumers don't know what they want until you show it to them.

Could both views be right?

Do workers choose the hours they want to work, or do employers choose the workers who will work in the patterns they prefer? Is the sharing economy a great opportunity to increase the efficiency of our economy, reduce our use of natural resources and create a stream of additional revenue for some workers? Or is it a new tool of oppression that will see workers' pay and conditions cut, and ultimately rip consumers off?

Like the binary question of whether we should have more economic activity or less, questions like these probably do more to maintain the status quo than they do to help us understand it. Worse, their paralysing effect might simply create room for people with no concern for workers or the environment to shape the regulations and cultural norms that will ultimately settle such questions.

The potential to lighten the load our economy places on the natural environment is enormous. But the premise of this book is not that technology will *fix* everything, but that technology and culture can and will *change* everything. The pace and direction of that change, like the rope in a tug-of-war, will be determined by the relative strength of the forces pulling on it.

Attempts to radically reshape the patterns of consumption, and in turn the world of work, inevitably come with risks. But recent history suggests that maintaining the status quo is even more likely to harm the most vulnerable members of our community. And the natural environment simply cannot support the exponential growth in consumption that, unless we change course radically, is coming down the line.

Every citizen, community and country has the capacity to lighten the load that their economic activity places on the natural environment. Every law passed by parliaments and local councils, and every decision made by consumers, has the potential to *reshape* the economy. If billions of people consciously sought to pursue a lighter-weight economy, they could achieve that goal. Those in the supply chain who profit from selling the products that weigh most heavily on our environment and society will, inevitably, fight against such change; it would be irrational for them not to. But the idea that we should keep burning coal in order to keep coalmines profitable makes about as much sense as encouraging people to keep buying things they don't need, just to make the economy strong. Oh, wait ...

John Quiggin

Since the dawn of history (literally, of written records), civilisation has depended critically on paper. As living standards have risen, so has the volume of paper produced, printed and read. The more knowledge we have and the wider its distribution, the more paper is needed.

At least, that was true until the end of the twentieth century. With the rise of the internet, the correlation between paper and information broke down. Increasingly, information is created and manipulated in electronic form, with paper serving mainly as an official record of the process.

In 2013 the world reached Peak Paper. World production and consumption of paper reached its maximum, flattened out, and is now falling. In fact, the peak in the traditional use of paper, for writing and printing, took place a few years earlier, but was offset for a while by continued growth in other uses, such as packaging and tissues.

Peak Paper highlights the meaninglessness of using traditional measures of economic growth to measure growth in an information-based economy. Consider, for example, the assumption that resource inputs, economic outputs and the value of those outputs are all related to each other in 'fixed proportions'. This implies it is reasonable to expect that if input use is growing, output will be growing, and if input use is shrinking, output will be shrinking. Until the end of the twentieth century, such assumptions worked reasonably well for the relationship between paper production, the number of books and newspapers consumed and the value of the information they transmitted. The volume of information grew somewhat more rapidly than the economy as a whole, but not so rapidly as to undermine the notion of an aggregate rate of economic growth.

Throughout this period, the volume of printed books, newspapers and so on grew steadily, to around a million new books every year. In total, Google estimates that 130 million different books have been published throughout history. The demand for paper for printing grew in line with that for books.

In the twenty-first century, these relationships have broken down. On the one hand, as we have seen, the production and consumption of paper has slowed and declined. On the other hand, there has been an explosion in the production and distribution of information of all kinds. The growth of information has passed the point where measurement is feasible, but almost certainly justifies Google founder Eric Schmidt's 2010 estimate that 'every two days we create as much information as we did up to 2003'.

Peak Paper is not an isolated example. Thanks to a combination of energy efficiency and innovations in renewable energy, the world has already passed Peak Coal. Self-driving electric vehicles seem likely to bring Peak Oil, not because we are going to run out of oil but because it will cease to be valuable enough to find and extract.

The case of Peak Steel is even more interesting. Steel lasts a long time and can be recycled almost endlessly, but demand is finite. In developed countries the stock of steel reached about eight tonnes per person decades ago, and has remained stable or declined slowly since then. With the stock of steel on a gently sloping plateau, the need for more can be met almost entirely by recycling scrap, rather than by burning coal to smelt iron ore in blast furnaces. Peak Steel may not be imminent, but it is achievable.

Contrary to what alarmists on both sides of the growth debate have often claimed, these developments do not imply a reduction in living standards or an end to the process of economic development. Rather, the information economy in which we are now living allows us to break the link between improving living standards and unsustainable growth.

In the process, we have the chance to realise some of the most appealing aspects of the 'degrowth' idea proposed by the Club of Rome in the 1970s. The information economy allows us to abandon the twentieth-century social model in which adults spend most of their days in an organised workplace. Instead, much of the value in the information economy is generated by informal interactions through various forms of social media. Combining this trend with steadily increasing productivity makes it possible to imagine a massive reduction in formal working hours, perhaps to the fifteen hours a week envisaged by Keynes nearly a century ago.

Professor John Quiggin is the author of _Zombie Economics_ and maintains a blog at johnquiggin.com.

4.

Your Country Needs You
(to work less, if you want to)

Unemployment doesn't scare the rich; in fact, it is their goal. Most of the British royal family haven't worked for centuries. While a stint in the military might be acceptable for some of them, nothing would shame a British royal more than a life spent selling real estate or working in a post office. Is going to a charity ball really 'tireless work for the disadvantaged'? Actually, cleaning the toilets after the ball is the tireless work. The idea that work is required to give people dignity clearly doesn't apply to everyone.

There is no economic difference between retiring early and unemployment: the difference is purely one of status, attitude and material comfort. Of course, 'early retirement' is not the only term used to describe those who don't need to work to meet their material and psychological needs; others include 'man of leisure', 'playboy' and 'of independent means'. The persistent wealth gap between men and women means it is no coincidence that the terms describing the indolent rich are so gendered; nor is it by chance that many terms which do describe women imply some link to a man – for example, 'kept woman'.

After more than 200 years of rapid economic growth, it should come as no surprise that countries can afford to maintain a class of consumers who have no need to produce anything. Indeed, what is surprising is that, in a democracy, there has been so little pressure for a larger proportion of the population to be admitted to this non-working class. (While more comprehensive wealth taxes and death duties would solve the problem quite quickly, these suggestions are usually dismissed as 'mere populism' by those determined to depict reasonable policy change as radically unrealistic.)

Daily toil and the risk of starvation dominated the minds of the majority of humans throughout recorded history, but this changed in the twentieth century. At the beginning of that century, an average worker in the United States worked about 59 hours per week, and by 1970 this figure had fallen to 41 hours per week.[16] The pursuit by organised labour of the eight-hour day, weekends and annual holidays all helped minimise the unemployment that accompanied the steady mechanisation of labour over that period.

The dirty secret of economics is that productivity growth – the ability to produce more output from the same amount of input – is a direct cause both of rises in living standards *and* of rapid job destruction. One of the biggest reasons for the disconnect between what most economists think is good for society and what most other people think is good for society is that economists focus on how machines free people from toil in the long run, while people tend to focus on how machines free people from jobs (and thus from their sources of income) in the short run. Making things better in the long run can be a worthy goal, but, as Keynes famously said, in the long run we are all dead.

Let's look at some examples. There is no doubt that the invention of tractors displaced a lot of farm workers. Online hotel booking has meant fewer jobs for receptionists in hotels across the world. Driverless vehicles will destroy taxi- and truck-driving jobs in the decades to come.

The disappearance of some people's jobs in this way isn't all bad. Few workers yearn for the days when teams of people – always low-paid, sometimes even slaves – toiled for long hours in the fields with heavy tools, and yet produced less food per acre than a single modern farmer in an air-conditioned tractor can produce. But nor is productivity growth always good. Just because new technologies such as Uber have the capacity to increase productivity (by matching people with spare time and cars to people with no car who need to go somewhere), that doesn't mean the result is unambiguously beneficial for society. This is especially the case when a new technology can be used not just to navigate city streets, but also to avoid important tax, employment and workplace safety obligations. Similarly, the fact that broadacre farming allows for far more food production, per worker and per acre, in the short term, doesn't mean that the land, water or natural environment can sustain the intensive production techniques used in the long term.

Any country that banned tractors could create a lot of labouring jobs in agriculture. A country that banned bulldozers could create a lot of jobs in road building and construction. Indeed, there are plenty of low-income countries in which roads are built with a lot more shovels and a lot less machinery than in the developed world. But few people, and even fewer economists, would advocate such an approach to job creation.

What is missing from our debates about technological change and job loss is the fundamentally cultural issue of *how* the benefits of new technologies, and the remaining work, should be distributed. In a society in which income is (for most non-royals, at least) directly linked to the amount of work one performs, using technology to 'free' people from toilsome tasks is the very same thing as depriving them of their income.

From 1900 to 1970, deliberate steps were taken across Western economies to ensure the shrinking amount of physical work was shared more evenly. The eight-hour day, the two-day weekend, paid public holidays and paid annual leave didn't just happen. They were the result of decades of campaigning by unions – campaigns that were often fiercely opposed by employers.

Today, though, at a time of rapid technological disruption (also known as productivity growth), job shedding in labour-intensive industries is taking place at the same time that work hours lengthen and holidays diminish. Put simply, the cultural preference for working longer hours and taking fewer holidays is worsening inequality and unemployment.

Redistributing work has the inevitable consequence of redistributing income. If a million people chose to have a three-day weekend, the equivalent of 200,000 full-time jobs would be created.

But redistribution relates to tasks as well as time. When a company sacks administrative staff and pays its middle managers a bit more money to work longer hours, it increases income inequality in a society in which it is often claimed that no low-skilled jobs are available. The fact is there are low-skilled jobs that need to be done, but increasingly we expect more highly skilled workers to perform them, along with the high-skilled aspects of their jobs. (A side effect: this makes high-skilled workers less productive.)

Most of us could work shorter hours, and it would benefit all of us to do so. Our decision not to do so is as much cultural as personal. It has nothing to do with economics.

THE MAP IS NOT THE TERRITORY

Like explorers setting out for unfamiliar territory, voters, business leaders and policy-makers wish that someone had made a map that could help them prepare for the journey and guide them once they were underway. But just as no explorer can map a land they have never seen, so too can no economist or futurist map a future that has not yet arrived.

This doesn't mean no one tries, of course. As with all things economic, the best way to understand the future is to understand the past.

Spectacularly wrong though they often were, there was an honesty to the early maps of the world. Having carefully (if erroneously) mapped the relative size and distances of known rivers, mountains, towns and streams, cartographers would depict the 'end of the world', often with dragons and sea monsters, which simultaneously served to signal the finite knowledge the map contained and to discourage people from wandering too far afield.

Economic models are attempts to map the economy. They try to show the relative size of its different parts, and the links between them. Like a map, economic models can help us plan a journey – not one to new places, but into a new future. Perhaps even a future with lower taxes, fewer coalmines, more driverless cars or higher wages.

Unlike primitive maps, the primitive economic models we use today have no dragons around the edges to remind us of the limits of our knowledge. Rather than admit there are limits to how far they can see (hint: not very), economic modellers churn out fat reports full of fifty-year predictions about employment in specific industries, and the predictions are often precise to two decimal places. Modelling commissioned by the Minerals Council of Australia, for example, once attracted front-page media coverage with its prediction that the introduction of a modest carbon tax would result in the loss of 23,510 jobs over a twenty-year period.[17] Not 23,530, mind you – that would be an exaggeration. Exactly 23,510.

Despite the appalling track record of economic forecasters, there is usually nothing vague or imprecise about the predictions that the economic modellers make. That is not an accident. Commercial economic modellers know what their clients want, and their clients know that the public confuses *precision* with *accuracy*.

All economists have a terrible track record of predicting the future (myself included). None of our models comes close to the sophistication of the models used to predict the weather or how fast a plane that is yet to be built will fly through the air. Not only did economists fail to predict the global financial meltdown in 2008, many of the most prominent economists in the world confidently predicted there would be no such meltdown. And then, when they were wrong about that, they confidently predicted the recession wouldn't last long. And then, when the economy was slow to recover after an event they said would never occur, they offered advice about how best to fix things. In reflecting on the failure of economists and regulators, the former head of the US Federal Reserve Bank said, 'We had been lulled into a state of complacency.'[18] One of the main reasons we are advised to ignore the scientific warnings about the dangers of climate change is that some in the economics community actually argue that the cost of reducing greenhouse-gas emissions is too high, relative to the benefits of preventing dangerous climate change.

Economic modellers have absolutely no capacity to predict what will be invented in the next fifty years, or even the next five. They have no idea how the costs of different technologies will change over time, nor do they have the capacity to predict how consumer tastes and preferences will evolve over time.

And because the main driver of economic growth is new investment in the factories required to produce new things, economic models simply can't help us predict which parts of the economy will grow and which parts will shrink.

Imagine that in 1980 you asked an economist to model the 2018 economy. Given that her starting point would be the economy in 1980, and the way the different parts of the economy interacted with each other then, her model would have no mobile phones in it. And therefore no mobile phone manufacturing jobs, no mobile phone retail jobs, no mobile phone repair jobs, no mobile phone bills for consumers, and very little demand for lithium (a key ingredient in mobile phone batteries).

Now, imagine you asked an economist in 1990 to do the same thing. You couldn't have emailed him your request, as almost nobody outside the defence and science communities used email until 1994. Like his colleague from 1980, an economist in 1990 would try to build a picture of the future through what he knew of the present, and like his 1980 colleague he would fail to capture not just the rapid growth in the mobile phone industry, but in the internet industry as well. In 2017 the three biggest companies in the United States were Apple, Google and Microsoft. Like Amazon, Facebook, Twitter and Alibaba, none of them were big employers in 1980; most of them didn't even exist.

If we wanted our economic models to help policy-makers and the public think about the future – rather than helping the status quo defend itself from policy change for a few more years – we would include the computational equivalent of dragons at the edge of our known world. That is, we should model the existence of the unknown, and not pretend that the sectors of the economy we have today will be the only sectors of the future economy. Modellers' predictions about the future should, therefore, include an estimate of the number of people who will work in jobs that haven't been invented yet.

While it may seem scary, disappointing or even absurd to think that in the future most of us will work in jobs and industries that haven't yet been invented, it is the only honest prediction we can make. If someone in 1917 had accurately predicted that employment in agriculture in 2017 would fall from 30 per cent of the labour force to 3 per cent, you can imagine that agricultural workers would have been sufficiently alarmed to resist any technological changes to farming. But how many people in wealthy countries today see themselves as unemployed farmers and yearn for a return to hard, low-paid work with shovels and hoes?

Only when we freely admit that we have no capacity to predict the future of the economy will we be able to begin to plan for it in a meaningful way. And only when we admit how destructive productivity growth can be to the lives of individuals will we acknowledge the need for society to provide generous, constructive support to those made unemployed by technological change.

ONLY THE PAST CAN HELP US UNDERSTAND THE FUTURE

Those under the age of thirty may not know what I'm talking about, but no economist knew whether Beta would prevail over VHS, DVD over LaserDisc, or Facebook over Myspace. But while economists have no particular skill in forecasting more than a year ahead, we *can* help people and politicians understand the causes and consequences of technological change and 'technological lock-in'.

Once a technology gets a head-start over its rivals, it can become unstoppable. Perhaps the most famous example of technological lock-in is the QWERTY keyboard. Early typewriters had a wide range of layouts, with some even going for the crazy option of alphabetical order. But once a critical mass of people had learned to touch-type on a QWERTY keyboard layout, or bought a VHS video recorder instead of Beta, their rivals fell by the wayside as typists (which was once a common job) refused to learn how to use two keyboards, and video libraries (once a big employer) refused to stock two formats of every film.

Economists can explain the theory of lock-in, the significance of critical mass and the way that, once a technology gets a lead over its rivals, the 'economies of scale' that come with mass production allow it to undercut its competitors on price. But what economists can't predict is *which* technology will prevail. We can only explain, in retrospect, why one product prevailed over the other. Like 'Monday-morning quarterbacks', economists pretend to know exactly why things that have already happened were inevitable.

While recent history tells us Facebook's growth and usurpation of Myspace was unstoppable, a longer view tells us that all unstoppable forces will ultimately be stopped. Just as surely as the CD manufacturers crushed the cassette tape, music streaming services destroyed not just the CD industry, but most shop-front music stores as well. Email destroyed the fax machine industry, spell-check software devastated pocket dictionary sales, and tablets and laptop computers have sent desktop computer sales plummeting. All of these changes have both created and destroyed jobs and industries.

Yet none of these changes was anticipated by economic modellers, and no 'structural adjustment' packages were ever provided to help the unemployed fax machine workers of the world. While the occurrence of economic change is easy to predict, its direction and timing are impossible to know in advance.

There have, of course, been much larger shifts in consumer preferences in the past 200 years than the shift from fax to email. The Industrial Revolution began with the shift from no engines to steam engines. As with the shift to email, the result was a massive increase in productivity, a massive reduction in the cost of living and massive displacement of workers across the rapidly mechanising agriculture and manufacturing sectors. While falling prices for food and manufactured stuff eventually led to a rise in demand for these things, and many more people were eventually employed in factories as a result, the 'transition' for the unemployed labourers was as harsh as it was undeserved. That so little of the profits from the new factories were redistributed to the displaced workers is an indictment of the tax and welfare policies of the day, not of the shift from shovels to tractors.

While the move from steam engines to internal-combustion engines was more gradual than the shift from horses to steam, it was no less devastating for those whose skills or capital were tied up in the production of boilers, valves and pistons. Diesel trains needed far fewer people to fuel them than did the steam trains they replaced, and just as electric trains required far less maintenance than diesel trains (and produced a lot less pollution in crowded cities), the handful of moving parts in electric cars will soon destroy the business model of car dealers and mechanics, which has been built up over the last 100 years.

The last whaling ship sailed out of Australia's Byron Bay in 1962.[19] Whale oil was once the 'cleanest' form of internal lighting, and around the world the hunting of whales, the refining of the huge quantities of oil they held in their heads, and the retailing of that oil was an enormous and profitable industry. But the electric light was brighter and cheaper, and required far fewer people to produce it.

Electric refrigeration was named by the US National Academy of Engineering as one of the most important inventions of the twentieth century. It was also responsible for the rapid destruction of one of the world's most traded commodities. Giant chunks of ice were once carved from Arctic lakes and moved around the world in ships lined with sawdust and hay. Ice was even ferried as far south as Sydney and Cape Town.

As the size and profitability of the Arctic ice-harvesting industry boomed, the threat from 'artificial ice' was seen as remote and trivial. Given that thousands of ships were dedicated to the task of moving ice around the world, the prospect of commercial production of ice was of some, but not much, concern to ship owners. As *The American Ship* magazine explained in 1880: 'Ice machines would be as useful in supplying New York as a boy's squirt gun at a fire. Running full time, one of them can make six tonnes per day, while requirements of a single company in the summer season are 250 tonnes per day.'[20]

Like the owners of coal-fired power stations today, those who profited by selling ice convinced themselves that there was little chance of a competitor becoming cheaper and more convenient. As Upton Sinclair once quipped, 'It is difficult to get a man to understand something, when his salary depends upon his not understanding it.'

By the start of World War I, the Arctic ice-harvesting industry was beginning to collapse under pressure from new steam-powered artificial ice-making machines; they were no longer squirt guns but garden hoses. Yet it was the emergence of the humble household electric refrigerator that really destroyed the natural ice industry, and in so doing transformed the world. It made food cheaper and safer to transport and store, and largely created the processed-food industry we know today. The electric refrigerator simultaneously destroyed the livelihoods of hundreds of thousands of people whose incomes revolved around the natural ice trade, and made fortunes for some manufacturers, farmers and retailers.

The pace of the transition from no fridges to lots of fridges was staggering. In 1926 only 2000 household refrigerators were sold in the United States; by 1937 an estimated 3 million had been installed.[21] No economic model could have predicted the shifts to steam, electricity or refrigeration, nor could any model have anticipated the huge growth in employment that electrification, refrigeration and internal-combustion engines would create. Without cars, there would have been no caravans, no caravan factories, no caravan parks and no grey nomads.

Although we have no capacity to predict the composition or size of the economy in ten or 100 years, history assures us that it will not look much like today's. Change is the only constant, and how we adapt to change is the most important challenge we face. No democratic government can decide which new industries will emerge and which old ones will decline, but all governments can decide whether they will be kind or cruel to those thrown from their jobs by the turmoil that we call 'technological change' or 'productivity growth'. No democratic government can mandate the direction in which new technologies – and, in turn, whole industries – will evolve, but all governments can influence the pace of the transitions and how the costs of change are shared among people and across communities.

With the rise of neoliberalism in the 1980s, the desire of governments to intervene and help workers and communities adjust to change diminished sharply. However, the recent voter backlash against rising inequality, which has delivered the Brexit movement, the unexpected electoral success of Donald Trump, and nationalism in countries such as Australia, Sweden and France, has forced a significant rethink of this. Just as the Russian Revolution in 1917 led to a more enthusiastic embrace of income redistribution by other European aristocracies, the rise of economic nationalism around the world has forced organisations such as the World Bank and the IMF to admit that there might just be a few more policy options than they had previously admitted. It is now rare to hear business leaders or politicians declare that 'there is no alternative'.

HARMING THE ENVIRONMENT WON'T GUARANTEE JOB SECURITY

In a country with low unemployment benefits where it can take months, even years, to find a new job after you have been retrenched, it makes sense to fear losing your job. But what makes no sense is the belief, deliberately propagated by the extractive industries and many politicians, that the more harm we do to the environment, the more jobs, and the higher quality jobs, we will create. With robot trucks and robot logging machinery it is, of course, becoming increasingly possible to do enormous environmental harm while creating almost no jobs whatsoever.

Whether countries rapidly transform their energy and transport sectors to reduce greenhouse-gas emissions or not, hundreds of millions of people around the world will likely lose their jobs in the coming decades as a result of new technologies, such as robots, artificial intelligence and 3D printing. While history suggests hundreds of millions of jobs will be created in new industries we can't imagine yet, history also tells us the transition will not be smooth or fair.

Put simply, regardless of a country's willingness, or reluctance, to reduce greenhouse-gas emissions, its workforce will experience enormous amounts of job shedding and job creation in the coming decades. While robot trucks and robot doctors attract lots of attention, in reality robot welders have already replaced vast amounts of people in the car industry, and online hotel booking algorithms have already replaced huge numbers of receptionists, travel agents and call-centre workers.[22]

There is perhaps no more ironic example of how phoney the 'jobs versus environment' debate is than the coal industry. The burning of coal is the single largest cause of greenhouse-gas emissions in the world, yet not only does the industry have a tiny workforce, that workforce has been shrinking rapidly as a result of improvements in technology. In an open-cut coalmine more people are now employed to drive trucks than to perform any other task, and the latest generation of mines is already using robot-controlled trucks.

Put simply, the coalmining industry is simultaneously standing in the way of new (renewable) electricity generation technologies while spending up big to develop new (highly automated) coal extraction technologies. The mining companies' own annual reports make clear that they are planning to increase fossil fuel production while reducing the size of their workforces. And the kicker is, they have the chutzpah to blame environmentalists for the job losses. While environmentalists often plead for effective climate policy on the basis that 'there are no jobs on a dead planet', it seems the coal industry is keen to ensure that there aren't even any jobs on a dying planet.

Between 1987 and 2002 the Australian coalmining industry shed half its workforce.[23] These enormous job cuts devastated local mining communities, but they were not the result of radical changes by government in environmental policy: they came simply from the pursuit of profit. Changes in technology and the law allowed for a shift away from the relatively labour-intensive process of underground coalmining, and towards the open-cut mines that now scar the planet. While the Australian coalmining industry has, over the last twenty years, doubled its output, and the environmental harm it does, it now provides even fewer jobs.[24]

Yet the idea that harming the environment is necessary if we are to achieve low unemployment is central to the political strategy of those who profit from causing climate change. Take, for example, the proposed Adani Carmichael mine in Queensland. At full capacity, it will produce 60 million tonnes of coal per year.[25] When burned, this coal will release more than 120 million tonnes of carbon dioxide into the atmosphere.[26] Over its planned sixty-year life, the mine's proponents aim to produce 2.3 billion tonnes of coal. Emissions from the mine – extracting, transporting and then burning its coal – will release the equivalent of more than 4.7 billion tonnes of carbon dioxide.

The pits of the proposed Adani Carmichael mine, if laid end to end, would be 40 kilometres long and 10 kilometres wide. If they started at the base of the Eiffel Tower, a person standing at the top of the tower would not be able to see their end. But although the surface area of the mine would be three times the size of metropolitan Paris, the mine would, according to the developer, create a maximum of 1400 jobs. If all those jobs go to people who are currently unemployed, the result would be a 0.01 per cent reduction in Australia's unemployment rate.

The potential for fixing unemployment by causing climate change is even lower in the United States and the United Kingdom. While less than 0.5 per cent of Australians work in coalmining, in the US and UK it is 0.03 per cent and 0.01 per cent respectively.[27] But while the fossil-fuel industry accounts for only a tiny fraction of the world's jobs, it is one of the most profitable industries in the world. So, just as Luddite workers once jammed their spanners into machinery to slow down the shift from manual to mechanised production, the fossil-fuel industry now seeks to jam its lobbyists into the political process to slow down the global trend to limit burning of fossil fuels.

Fossil-fuel companies are not naive enough to think that saving their profits will be seen as a good reason to avoid dangerous climate change. So instead they feign concern for the workers who could lose their jobs. But history provides clear evidence that the expansion of environmentally harmful activities does not guarantee more jobs. Indeed, it is possible for that expansion to *cost* jobs. For example, the enormous Adani Carmichael mine will be automated 'from pit to port'. If it goes ahead, it will take business from other, more labour-intensive mines. Put simply, as well as causing climate change, building enormous new coalmines can cause unemployment. The fact is that the vast majority of workers in the coal industry are destined to lose their jobs whether or not the world limits its greenhouse-gas emissions.

But the fact that workers in the coal industry, and a wide range of other industries, will lose their jobs as technology and culture change doesn't mean that individuals or countries should be indifferent to their plight. On the contrary! If – and it is a big if – governments are concerned about the plight of coal workers, or video-store workers, or fax-machine workers, any workers at all, they should focus on helping such workers and the regions where they live.

DON'T LOOK AT THE TIGER, LOOK AT THE MAGICIAN

Magicians love to take to the stage alongside tigers, scantily clad assistants or flames shooting from the floor. Sometimes they go for all three. It's a great way to distract people from the sleight of hand. The same is true of conservative politicians and business leaders talking about the labour market.

Each month in the United States, around 3 million people leave their jobs, either voluntarily or involuntarily. Luckily, in an average month, around 3 million people also find a new job so, despite the huge 'churn' in the labour market, the overall number of unemployed people tends to change only slightly each month. The same pattern is evident in all developed countries. But this churn is so common that it doesn't receive media attention. What is more likely to be reported is the closure or opening of a large or somehow symbolic factory, mine or shopping centre.

There is no doubt that the closure of a factory and the loss of 300 jobs in a community is devastating for those who are sacked and their families. But there is also no doubt that when a local bakery closes down and three people lose their job, it is devastating for them and their families as well. Only after you accept that millions of people lose their jobs in a country the size of the USA every month can you start to conceive of the full horror of mass unemployment.

While the media focus on large factories suddenly shutting down is understandable, the picture it paints of the labour market helps neither citizens nor policy-makers understand how the economy really works, and what really causes (or fixes) unemployment. While averting premature factory closures is obviously of benefit to those who work in them, the idea that unemployment can be significantly reduced by preventing the closure of symbolically important workplaces is as dangerously misconceived as suggesting that the biggest threat to workers' job security is the effort to reduce greenhouse gases. Indeed, often far more workers are required to clean up a coalmine or disused factory than to operate one. Reshaping economic activity in ways that reduce environmental harm can help to create jobs in a multitude of ways. Imagine, for example, if environmentalists and unionists succeeded in persuading governments to spend up big to construct a large amount of renewable energy capacity, to invest heavily in public transport infrastructure and to build new schools, hospitals and aged-care homes. The result would be a significant increase in economic activity, measured as an increase in GDP, and a reduction in the level of unemployment.

Surely investing in renewable energy and public transport can't be bad for the environment?

And surely if building new coalmines creates jobs, then building new wind turbines and hospitals must create jobs as well?

The apparent 'paradox' that higher rates of economic growth can help both the environment and the unemployed is easy to resolve. What matters is not the amount of economic activity, but its composition. If it is the parts of the economy that do little or no harm to the natural environment that are doing the growing, then an increase in economic activity will have little or no impact on the environment. And if the parts of the economy that are doing the growing are more labour-intensive than average, then an increase in economic activity will help reduce unemployment. (Alternatively, if the kinds of economic activity that are growing rapidly are highly capital-intensive, or require only robots, then it is quite possible to have 'jobless growth'.)

Put simply, if we want to help the environment without harming workers, then we need to focus not on the level of economic activity, but on how it is composed and distributed.

WE NEED A JUST ECONOMY

Less than 2 per cent of the world's workers are employed in the extraction of fossil fuels. Even in mining regions, it is rare that direct employment in mining exceeds 10 per cent And in the decades to come, it is difficult to imagine that more than 2 per cent of workers will be directly employed in the production of renewable energy. To put those figures in perspective, in the United States the health sector employs around 11 per cent of the workforce, and manufacturing – which many believe has collapsed – employs 8.5 per cent.[28] And, as discussed, around 3 million workers are moving into and out of jobs in the USA each month. The same pattern of far more people working in health than in the manufacturing or energy sectors is common across nearly all developed economies.

The vast majority of people who lose their jobs in the coal and oil industries – either as a result of government policy or after being replaced by robots – will not be re-employed in green jobs, such as making wind turbines or solar panels. Like the vast majority of all workers, those who lose their jobs in these fossil-fuel industries will find new work in the 96 per cent of jobs that are unrelated to energy production.

Indeed, in twenty years' time, far more of today's coal and oil workers will work in industries that don't yet exist than the number who will continue to work in the fossil-fuel or renewable energy industries. The same is true of the hundreds of millions of people who will lose their jobs – through no fault of environmentalism – in the finance, retail and transport sectors.

The visceral fear of unemployment felt by those who did not inherit significant wealth makes sense, especially in countries such as the United States, Australia and the United Kingdom, which have largely chosen to treat the unemployed punitively. But this fear cannot be allayed by the expansion of the fossil-fuel industry or any other industry that is causing significant social or environmental harm. There are only two ways to reduce the fear that so many people have of unemployment:

- Use expansionary macroeconomic policies (that's econobabble for using budgetary policies and interest rates) that have been proven to cause economic growth and keep unemployment down.

- Provide generous support to those who are unemployed as a result of macroeconomic, regional, sectoral or personal circumstances.

The causes of and solutions for unemployment have been the source of at least 300 years of sustained economic debate and the debate is unlikely to be resolved in the next 100 years, or the next 100 pages. But in the whole history of economic debate the idea that a good way to create jobs is to allow, or to even subsidise, activities that do harm to people and the planet (sometimes called 'goods with negative externalities') is an entirely new one. I am even going to go as far as to say that the argument that harming the environment is a necessary or effective way to help the unemployed isn't even an economic argument, it's just complete bullshit.

Just as there is no way to deliver job security to all the world's workers over the coming decades, there is no factory, industry or region which, if protected for long enough, will prevent economy-wide unemployment from occurring. Unemployment will arise when cultural and technological change mean that the people who were once required to make one type of stuff are no longer required make that kind of stuff. Fashion and cultural change destroy far more jobs than environmental regulations. Mass unemployment will arise when the amount of goods and services bought by people is not sufficient to create enough work for all of the people looking for work. When mass unemployment exists, governments can create a lot of work by paying people to do important things such as build renewable energy or look after the sick and the old. They can collect more taxes from people who can afford to spend a lot of money on conspicuous consumption, or they can borrow money to be repaid after the mass unemployment has been exhausted. It is politics, not economics, and not environmentalism, that prevents the implementation of the Keynesian policies that worked so effectively in both the post-war period and, in some countries at least, after the global financial crisis.

Some powerful people are opposed to the pursuit of such an approach to full employment. They fear that they

might have to pay higher taxes, and they fear that without high unemployment workers might demand higher
wages and better conditions. And some of them think that
the last few decades have been the best the world has ever
known. But rather than admit that they don't see a problem with the way things are, many powerful people prefer
instead to suggest that unemployment is the fault of lazy
workers or greedy environmentalists. The most amazing
thing is that, to date, they have gotten away with it.

No one knows what the future holds for any particular industry, region or occupation. But science tells us
quite clearly what will happen if we fail to rapidly reduce
our global greenhouse-gas emissions. Just like the workers
who will inevitably lose their jobs in the coalmines (if only
because of the robots), those workers who lose their jobs
because of technological change, cultural change, regional
decline or simple bad luck deserve to be treated with dignity,
supported financially, helped with retraining or relocation,
and made to feel like valued members of the community.

Such an approach would not be unprecedented.
Countries such as Australia once prided themselves on
having this type of society; countries such as Sweden,
Norway and Denmark still do. If we treated all unemployed people with generosity and dignity, workers would
have no reason to fear change – and that, of course, is why
those seeking to maintain the status quo are determined
to keep them scared.

Jim Stanford

Work. It's a four-letter word. And it certainly feels that way on Monday mornings, as we drag ourselves out of bed and off to our jobs. Yet it's a necessity of life for almost all of society – for the simple reason that most of us have to work, just to support ourselves.

This love–hate relationship with work is as old as humanity. After all, productive human labour – using our brains and our brawn – to produce the goods and services we need to survive and thrive, has been the driving force of our economic progress since we first descended from the trees. Of course, work has changed constantly through the eons: how we work, the tools we use, what we produce and – crucially – how we organise our work. But 'work', broadly defined as productive human effort, has been a constant, and will remain so.

Recently, many have been concerned that work as we know it is disappearing. For some, this is due to a new wave of automation (including machine-learning technologies that allow the application of machinery to a wide range of non-standard and creative tasks). For others, it reflects the rise of digital business models, which enable employers to extract labour through temporary 'gigs' rather than lasting 'jobs'. Still others worry we have to cut back on work, to reduce the damage we're doing to an already polluted environment.

In my view, none of these factors will lead to the elimination of work. They *can't*. Because work is the fundamental source of value-added: it's the only thing that can transform the materials we harvest from nature (hopefully sustainably) into the full range of goods and services we need to live a full life. Not just big-screen TVs and throw-away dollar-store products. But also food, clothing and shelter; education and health care; entertainment, culture and community. All of it takes work.

Even in a highly automated economy, work is still the essential driving force of production. After all, it takes human labour (mental and physical) to invent the machinery, engineer it, manufacture it, operate it and maintain it. To be sure, new vistas in automation will eliminate many jobs currently performed by humans in the same way that tractors once displaced enormous numbers of farm labourers. At the same time, other jobs will be created through automation, including jobs doing new tasks we've never thought of before. There's no guarantee there will be enough new work, that it will be fairly distributed, that it will be decent work. (I am actually more concerned about the negative impact of technology on the *quality* of jobs, than on the *quantity* – given the current power of bosses to unilaterally implement and manipulate technology in ever-more exploitive and degrading ways.) But there will certainly be work.

Workers in digital 'gigs' (like Uber or Airtasker) are still workers. They're just not getting paid as well, or treated as fairly, as they would have in previous business forms. There's nothing new about exploitation. And there is nothing new about the need for new forms of regulation to protect workers in new forms of employment. Workers have banded together before to drive such change, in the face of both technological and social change. And while it's never easy, they can do it again.

As for the relationship between the need for work and the need to protect our natural environment, it's more obvious than ever that we actually have a *lot* of work to do to protect the environment: building green energy systems, public transit, implementing energy conservation and cleaning up all the pollution and harm that's already been done. The big question isn't whether there will be any jobs, but rather, how do we want work to be organised and motivated? How will the people performing the work be treated? What will we produce, and what will we do with it?

In recent decades we have grown accustomed to the idea that such questions will be answered by the owners of private, for-profit business. But that profit-led model leads to all kinds of problems, including unacceptable treatment of those doing the work and unacceptable environmental side effects from production. But this isn't the only way to organise work. In fact, we can imagine different ways of motivating and compensating work – to better ensure the work we do is useful, and the people doing it are treated fairly.

The deteriorating quality and stability of work typical of the modern precarious labour market is not inevitable. And it is not driven primarily by technology. It reflects the power of employers – in a context of inadequate work and weak employment regulations – to compel desperate people to work for less, under increasingly unfavourable and demeaning conditions.

Ultimately it is the collective choice of our society how work is going to be organised and compensated. There will be plenty of work to do in the coming century, but whether there are plenty of good jobs working to meet important community goals, and fair distribution of those jobs, is up for grabs. Through unions, community activism and legislative change, workers in the first half of the twentieth century reshaped their workplaces and communities. With effort and strategy, we can do so again this century.

Jim Stanford is an economist and director of the Centre for Future Work, and author of *Economics for Everyone: A Short Guide to the Economics of Capitalism*.

5.

Change Your Shape, Not Your Size

In 1961 US President John F. Kennedy decided he wanted to put a man on the moon. Eight years and 400,000 jobs later, the United States made that giant leap, showing that it is possible for a nation-state to do pretty much anything it puts its collective mind to.

However, after decades of being told that governments were inefficient and wasteful, when President George W. Bush announced in 2004 that the United States would put a person on Mars, no one cared and no one believed him. Cultures change. Tastes change. Goals change. And people, not markets, are responsible for those changes.

Rich countries can't afford to do everything they want, but they can afford to do virtually anything they want. For the past few decades, people have been told that it is the market that determines the shape of the economy. Indeed, people in many countries have even been told that they must sacrifice some things they want the government to do – such as provide high-quality publicly funded education – in order to keep the markets happy and make the economy strong. But, as we saw in Chapter 2, market forces no more want your kids to have a poor education than gravitational forces want you to fall off your bike.

The question of how big we want our national economies to be has drowned out the far more important question of what shape we want them to be. Few would decide on the number of new pieces of clothing they need and have no view about the style or size. But political and business leaders often declare that they want to 'grow the economy' without making any reference whatsoever to which of its parts they would like to see expand.

In recent decades, far too much time has been wasted debating whether economic growth is good or bad. We might as well debate whether sunshine is better than rain. What we can say is that when the good bits of an economy are growing, that's good. And when the bad bits are growing, that's bad. The democratic challenge is to have a meaningful debate about what constitutes 'good' and what constitutes 'bad'. And on that debate economists have surprisingly little to offer.

Voters are increasingly hostile to claims that the economy is growing strongly when their own experience is one of stagnating wages or rising local unemployment. They are right to be sceptical. Talking to people about the average rate of economic growth across their country is no more meaningful than telling them what the average rainfall across that country will be tomorrow. Even if the prediction is accurate, it won't be very useful: knowing the average national rainfall won't help anyone decide what to wear or whether to cancel their picnic.

Do you want your economy to have a big education sector or a big shopping mall sector? Do you want it to have a booming arts sector or a booming finance sector? These are choices that, over time and around the world, citizens have shaped. They are not choices made by 'the market' or 'globalisation'. They are choices made by people.

So what shape do you want your country's economy to be? What do you wish there was more of? What do you wish there was less of? What are your goals for your nation? As productivity grows and the capacity for the people in your economy to produce more output with fewer inputs rises, what do you want your kids or your grandkids to have that you didn't have?

Not sure? Maybe you should ask an expert. But what kind of expert would you consult?

ECONOMICS IS ABOUT THE HOW, NOT THE WHAT

No one asks their accountant what they should buy the kids for Christmas, so why would a society ask its economists what kind of world we should build?

The ultimate irony of neoliberalism is that it has simultaneously trained people to believe that while the preferences and desires of the individual are paramount (hence the 'need' for ten different brands of margarine), if individuals want to be part of a collective solution to a problem, they must be wrong. How can that be? How can it be right to give consumers the choice of so many types of margarine, but wrong for voters to opt for a public health system over a private one? Likewise, free marketeers think it's okay to let people decide whether or not to smoke in the presence of children, but apparently it's not okay for people to choose longer holidays over higher incomes. We either trust people to know what they want or we don't.

As we have seen, economics is primarily concerned with the efficient allocation of scarce resources. But it's concerned with means, not ends; it considers how to produce things efficiently, not what things to produce.

Like an accountant looking at your family's spending patterns, economists can help spell out the options we as a society face and the likely trade-offs for different courses of action. They can perhaps even give some broad advice about the kinds of spending that might deliver long-term benefits (such as preventive health) and those that will not (such as cigarette smoking).

But, like accountants, economists are unlikely to encourage you to spend up big on piano lessons for your child, or rounds of golf, or language classes, or any other of your kid's passions or hobbies. Instead they might argue that a more sensible investment is to deposit the cost of such 'luxuries' into a bank account each week and then hand your child a nice cheque on their twenty-first birthday.

And why stop there? What if your family never took a holiday, and deposited the money you didn't spend into a savings account as well? And what's with spending weekends together? If you and your partner worked part-time jobs at the weekend, imagine how much money you could salt away over the years. Such decisions might be deemed sensible by your accountant or economist, but to what end? You can see why most people don't rely on their accountant for advice beyond minimising their tax bill.

So to the all-important question: what is to be done? As a society, should we aim to spend more time with friends and family, or work longer hours and make more stuff? Should we provide free drinking water in all public spaces, or should we encourage people to buy bottled water? Should we require cars in our cities to be quiet and emit no air pollution, or should we let people drive anything they want?

All these questions have economic consequences, but none of them is an economic question. Yet we are often told that the right answer to such questions is to work longer hours, drink bottled water and drive cheap and polluting cars, because such choices are 'good for the economy'.

The idea that we must make personal and community sacrifices to 'help the economy' is a bizarre inversion of the socialist dictum that the needs of the individual are secondary to the needs of society. While encouraging people to work long hours and take fewer holidays will inevitably lead to an increase in economic activity, the idea that individuals have a social obligation to spend less time with their family than they want, and in turn to spend more money on stuff than they want, is a strange approach to the 'individualism' typically favoured by the political Right.

The fact that working long hours and buying lots of stuff leads to an increase in economic activity makes such a goal no more economically efficient than digging lots of holes and filling them back in. It's a task, not a goal. Put simply, the job of imagining the future is not for economists, but for scientists, engineers, artists, entrepreneurs and those who seek elected office. And the task of selecting the future options that we pursue in a functioning democracy is for every citizen, every day.

CULTURE CREATES JOBS

A lot of people want to know where the jobs of the future will be created. Kids want to know what training to undertake, investors and managers want to invest in industries before they boom, and politicians want to know who will be powerful in the future so they can start being nice to them in advance.

But, as we saw in Chapter 4, the simple fact is that no one knows what the future will look like. Not just because no one can predict what technologies will be invented, but also, and more fundamentally, because no one can predict how our culture will evolve over time. It is culture that plays the major role in determining what is fashionable, which fads will take off and whether a country spends hundreds of billions of dollars on bottled water or personal trainers; aircraft carriers or public transport.

Most fundamentally, the economy can't decide what kind of jobs will be created for the simple reason that there is actually no such thing as 'the economy'. You can touch a shop, you can talk to a shop owner, and you will probably notice if you drop a $100 note, but if you go looking for the economy, you will never find it.

While it's obvious that individual shops, shop owners, currency, coalmines and other parts of the economy aren't 'planning the future' or 'creating the jobs of the future', there has been so much talk about the 'global economy' that you can forgive yourself if you missed a subtle but important point: the global economy is simply a metaphor used to describe the interactions between all the customers and all the shops and factories in the world.

Like our national character, our national economy is an idea. While we can reach out and touch some of our economy's composite parts, we can never see, or consult with, its collective whole. While you can see your neighbour's pool in Google Maps, despite its enormous size you will never be able to spot the 'national economy', no matter how hard you look. Like the strength of a nation's democracy or the state of national security, talk of the strength of an economy is an abstraction. While some of its parts are material, 'the economy' is not a material thing, it doesn't have a consciousness and it certainly doesn't make plans. This simple fact causes a lot of confusion about who is shaping our society, who is making decisions about the future and what the role of individual citizens in a democracy is.

Since World War II, economists and statisticians have worked hard to make their best estimate of the size of the economy, compiling the value added by billions of transactions each year. But despite the difficulty of the task, and the precision with which it is performed, an assertion like 'the economy grew by 2.7 per cent' is meaningless to a worker who has lost their job in a declining region, to a capitalist who has lost their investment in a declining industry, or to a politician who has lost their seat in a declining nation. And the fact that economic activity will grow as cities spend billions on sea walls to protect their citizens from rising oceans shows just how unrelated the measured size of the economy and the wellbeing of citizens can be.

When it comes to talking about the state of the economy averages can be unhelpful, to say the least. The average person has less than two legs, for instance. (There are far more people with no legs or one leg than there are people with three or four legs.) But it would be ridiculous to use this data to design trousers or staircases for the average citizen. Similarly, declaring that the economy grew by some particular amount last year conceals the fact that, in reality, millions of different citizens had millions of different experiences of the economy in that period. While there is some value in keeping track of national trends in the number and value of billions of transactions, there is no value in confusing the average growth rate of the economy with the lived experience of individuals.

Every time we spend a dollar, cast a vote, accept a job, donate to charity, quit a job, lobby a politician, switch banks, divest our retirement savings, plant some vegetables in the backyard or volunteer some time to a charity, we change the shape of the economy. Economic growth doesn't 'cause' investment in new factories or 'cause' consumers to spend more money. It is the money consumers spend on things that causes the owner of a factory to invest in expansion, which causes the measured size of the economy to grow. What actually matters for workers, communities and the environment is which bits are growing and which bits are shrinking.

A major reason why voters around the world are losing faith with traditional political parties and turning instead to populist alternatives is that they feel – quite correctly – that large parts of their national economy that they care about or rely on are going backwards, despite the official statistics suggesting that things are improving. Imagine if you had two kids and, having taken $20 from one of them and given $40 to the other, tried to argue that, on average, they were both $10 better off.

Knowing the average employment statistics or average wage growth across a country doesn't tell us whether our job is safe or our mortgage payments are getting easier to make. What affects an individual's job security and financial security is not some average of the 'idea' of the national economy but the circumstances in the places they actually live. Politicians who try to tell unemployed people in a declining region that 'the economy is doing well' will not only fail to persuade the unemployed to cheer up, they will likely enrage them.

Statistical indicators such as GDP and the national unemployment rate can provide useful information when used responsibly for the purpose for which they were designed. There is no doubt that a focus on national production helped the Allies win World War II and helped Europe to rapidly recover from that war. And there is no doubt that a surging national unemployment rate is a clear warning sign for a national government concerned about poverty and inequality. But history makes clear that it is possible to have jobless growth, and that economies can grow rapidly in ways that deliver all of the benefits to high-income earners and do nothing to improve those on low incomes. National economic indicators can act as an early warning system, or as a cover story for social and environmental harm. But it is not the indicators that are good or bad, it is the use to which they are put.

THE GREAT WALL IS MADE OF SMALL BRICKS

It's hard to fathom the scale of something as big as the Great Wall of China. The average house contains thousands of bricks, but the Great Wall is made from nearly 4 billion of them. In fact, there's nothing terribly special about these bricks – apart from their age. It's the collective structure that is so impressive. The global economy is much the same: its composite parts might seem insignificant on their own, but together they create something astounding.

The size and complexity of the global economy can be used to silence and demotivate individuals and groups pushing for change: how can you possibly affect something so enormous? But when you understand that it is nothing more than the sum of millions of local economies, you realise that if these local economies can change in ways that other communities might want to copy, then changing the global economy could be easier than it sounds. It is true that the decisions of individual consumers and individual companies have a minuscule impact on the global economy, but that's like saying being a good parent has a minuscule impact on global indicators of early childhood development, or that establishing a new farm will do nothing much to boost world food production. Such observations are true but meaningless.

The whole point of capitalism – and the whole reason that neoliberal economists claim to be so enthusiastic about capitalism – is that producers respond to changes in consumer tastes and preferences (often called 'shifts in demand'). So while individual changes in consumption are unlikely to have any effect, good or bad, on the world economy, or even on the national economy, it is also true that the major determinant of what most companies do, and of which companies survive, is the collective decision-making of individual consumers.

Once people realise that the 'national economy' and the 'global economy' exist only in the accounts of statisticians, the idea that the economy will create jobs for us – or that we need to work longer than we want to, or buy things we don't want in order to 'make the economy strong' – makes as much sense as sacrificing a goat to appease the gods.

If we want to stimulate (or curtail) the growth of a particular sector, there are only four things we can do:

- We can spend more (or less) of our disposable income on the goods produced by an industry.

- We can demand that the companies we buy things from buy more (or less) from an industry.

- We can demand that our elected representatives buy more (or less) from an industry.

- We can demand that our elected representatives make regulations that require more (or less) of an activity to occur.

That's it. And the economy doesn't make any of those decisions; it responds to them. Sometimes it responds quickly, sometimes it responds partially and sometimes it doesn't appear to respond at all. But in the long run, when enough people change enough of their decisions, significant economic change inevitably occurs.

History shows us that change is inevitable – consider the whaling industry, the ice industry and, more recently, the renewable energy industry. But while history says you can't stop progress, politics is increasingly perfecting the art of slowing it down.

CULTURE, CARS AND CHANGING THE ENERGY SYSTEM

Cars are one of the most expensive forms of transport imaginable. Expensive cars are, not surprisingly, an even more expensive mode of transport than cheap cars. (The most profitable segment of the car industry, in fact, is the production of the most expensive cars, with one estimate suggesting that the profit margin on a Porsche was 18 per cent compared with 2.9 per cent for Volkswagen.[29]) Yet as anyone who commutes to work by car knows, the expense of car transport is no guarantee of convenience.

Most car owners take it for granted that their choice of car says something about them. Even those who deny that their car says anything about them are likely to believe that other people's cars say something about them.

Twenty years ago, few city dwellers thought they needed a large four-wheel drive vehicle to navigate city streets. Why would anyone spend a lot more money than they needed to, in order to own a vehicle that costs more to run, is harder to park and significantly increases your chances of reversing over a child? But despite the obvious downsides, and financial cost, 'sports utility vehicles' are among the most common vehicles on the road today.

Why? 'Sports cars' can signal independence from the need to transport a family, or wealth, or simply that the owner is always in a hurry. (Of course, they have very little to do with sport.) Large four-wheel drive vehicles can signal a preparedness to head for the hills, a love of the great outdoors or perhaps just an attitude that other cars should get out of the driver's way. In fact, you could probably argue that cars are much better at performing their symbolic function than they are at moving us quickly around a city.

Despite their high cost to buy, register and insure, on average a car is used for around 5 per cent of the day. The rest of the time it is parked. Some might say it is the parking of the car – outside a house, or out the front of a cafe, or out the front of the office – that is its primary function in many cases.

To be clear, there is no reason people shouldn't use their cars as symbols. Doing so makes as much sense as using a watch, a jacket, a handbag or a tattoo to tell the world, or yourself, something about who you think you really are. But we can learn a lot from the willingness of people to spend large amounts of money on an expensive form of transport. For instance, we can learn about how the interaction between symbolism, cultural change and consumer choice drives not just the shape and size of the economy, but, quite literally, the shape and size of our towns and cities.

As the compact cars that were common in the 1970s were replaced by SUVs, which can weigh up to 3500 kilograms – that's almost three and a half times the weight of the top-selling car in France, the Renault Clio – this drove demand for billions of tonnes of extra iron ore, coal, oil and other materials.[30]

Electric cars are not light. The Tesla Model S weighs in at 2108 kilograms, 550 kilograms of which is in the lithium-ion batteries.[31] While only 540,000 electric cars were sold in 2015, Tesla alone is planning to produce 500,000 cars per year by 2018 and the world market for electric cars is forecast to hit 8 per cent by 2020, and 35 per cent by 2040.[32] Just as electric refrigerators destroyed demand for cut ice and boosted demand for coal-fired electricity, demand for electric cars will devastate the demand for oil in the coming decades and cause a massive increase in demand for the materials used to make batteries.

But Tesla doesn't just make expensive electric cars; it also makes expensive electric batteries. And what is particularly interesting about the company is how differently economists, politicians and the public treat its two main products.

The Tesla S sells for more than twice the average price of a car, and far more again than most alternative forms of transport. But no one is surprised that people voluntarily elect to spend a lot more money on one kind of car than another. That's what cars are for! If we really just wanted cars to provide cheap transport, then we would only need a few mass-produced models that, as Henry Ford famously said, would come in any colour you want as long as it's black.

But while we can accept that the demand for Tesla cars is, in part at least, because they are so expensive and cool, when it comes to Tesla batteries for household electricity storage, economists, regulators and commentators are regularly surprised to learn that demand is growing rapidly, *even though they don't provide the cheapest source of electricity available.*[33] Can you believe it – people spending more than is absolutely necessary on a household product! Where will it end?

Electricity grids in most developed countries have typically been designed by engineers and economists. In turn, the principles of economic theory and engineering are clearly visible in debates about how to achieve 'least cost greenhouse-gas abatement', how to select the 'optimal energy mix' and how to manage the trade-off between the cost of electricity and security of supply.[34] In turn, for decades we have been told that there is nothing we can do to reduce greenhouse-gas emissions without ruining the economy, and it is a ridiculous idea that we would ever willingly pay a slightly higher price to get a product with perceived benefits. As anyone who has ever bought a bottle of water should understand, consumers do not always want the cheapest product on the market.

Few middle-class consumers choose to buy only the lowest-priced food, the cheapest clothes or the cheapest houses they can find. Yet many economists and politicians are surprised that a growing number of people are willing to spend more than the minimum possible amount to obtain a form of energy supply that they see as providing improved energy security and improved environmental outcomes. Possibly it also makes them feel cool, in the same way that their expensive cars, watches or tattoos do.

To be clear, there is a role for economists and engineers in helping to design our energy system, but while many economists and engineers have been very vocal in criticising what they see as excessive spending on renewable energy, those same 'rational' voices cautioning about undue haste in installing renewable energy are strangely silent about the undue haste, and financial waste, associated with mass adoption of enormous SUVs, huge houses and bottled water.

Visible acts with spill-over environmental benefits, such as driving electric vehicles and putting solar panels on domestic roofs, are sometimes mocked as 'virtue signalling' by some on the conservative side of politics, but those who express concern about such public displays of good citizenship seem unconcerned by people who engage in 'wealth signalling' via the purchase of luxury cars or other expensive consumer goods. As with the social pressure on people to work longer hours and buy more stuff, some on the Right seem keen to affirm personal displays of wealth and to demean personal displays of generosity. They know culture matters.

If hundreds of millions of middle-class consumers decided that installing solar panels on their houses was a better way to demonstrate their upward mobility than spending the same amount of money on luxury cars, granite kitchen benchtops or other discretionary displays of status, the world economy, and the global environment, would be radically transformed. No laws would have to be passed and no lobbyists overcome. Similarly, if millions of people painted the roofs of their houses white, their homes would be cooler in summer and use less energy; like the melting polar icecaps once did, they would reflect a significant amount of energy back into space. But everyone knows that no one paints their roof white … except in the Mediterranean, which is different, of course. In the Mediterranean, white roofs are 'traditional'.

As every firm who has spent millions on advertising knows, it is neither easy to direct cultural change, nor possible to ensure it. But cultures do change, and the consequences of those changes are the predominant influence on the shape of the economy.

BUT MULTINATIONAL COMPANIES RUN THE WORLD…

While intellectually important, the main role of debates about whether free markets are good or bad is to conceal from the public that all governments, of all political stripes, intervene in markets all the time.

President Franklin D. Roosevelt's decision to enter World War II had an enormous influence on the size and shape of the economy in the United States in the 1940s, as well as on the outcome of the war itself. On a smaller scale, as we have seen, Eleanor Roosevelt's decision to grow vegetables on the lawn of the White House also affected the shape of economic activity. When governments insist that seatbelts be installed in cars, they shape the demand for seatbelts; when they introduce tough air-quality standards, they shape demand for coal and oil; and when they ban activities such as whale hunting, the production of landmines or the digging of new coalmines, they have a significant influence on the production and consumption of whale meat, landmines and coal.

And when JFK decided that putting a man on the moon was to become a national priority, it wasn't as if the nation had no other problems that needed solving. Indeed, the next president, Lyndon B. Johnson, declared war on poverty; presumably, JFK saw this as sitting lower on the to-do list than beating the Russians to the moon.

In hindsight, the US$24 billion cost of the Apollo 11 mission accounts for a trivial proportion of the current US federal government debt of $19 trillion. If the money spent on the mission had been saved instead of spent, and the interest avoided, the US debt today would be around $18.66 trillion. Put another way, the cost of the moon landing is little more than a rounding error.

Of course, while landing people on the moon looks expensive, when compared to the cost of buying vitamin supplements or bottled water it is small beer. And compared to defence spending, it's a veritable bargain. When it comes to defence, it seems that democracies believe you can never have too much of a good thing. In 2016 the United States spent more on defence than the next eight largest spenders combined – that's China, Russia, Saudi Arabia, India, France, the UK, Japan and Germany put together.[35]

And in 2017 Donald Trump suggested that a 10 per cent increase was required. When political leaders really want to do something, they can always find the money.

There is no right answer to the question of how many scarce resources a country should dedicate to producing bottled water or buying military aircraft. But for most countries, it appears the answer is a lot more than zero. Economics might be all about the efficient allocation of scarce resources, but politics is all about the practice of allocating scarce resources in a way that facilitates re-election. While it's possible there is overlap between what is efficient and what will ensure re-election, it's far from certain. Much confusion about political decision-making flows from the determination of elected politicians to feign a concern about efficiency while really focusing on re-electability. When you appreciate that the least re-electable thing a politician can say is, 'I'm only supporting this idea because it will help me get re-elected,' it becomes obvious why so many politicians prefer to pretend that their decisions are made to help the economy. It's much safer than telling the truth.

But in democracies at least, voters do have the final say on which politicians get elected – even if they don't know with certainty how their representative will subsequently vote on key issues. And in a market economy, consumers have the final say on whether Beta defeats VHS, or whether electric cars outcompete petrol-powered cars – again, even if the choices they are offered are not fair or complete. In turn, individual citizens are able both directly (through their own spending choices) and indirectly (through democratic means) to influence the shape of economic activity in their town, state and country, and globally.

It is hardly radical to suggest that this power not only exists, but that it is widely used. Just as growing preferences for electric cars, espresso coffee and app-based games with 'in-app purchases' are resulting in significant shifts in employment and production, the election of Donald Trump will result in a significant increase in public-sector spending on defence equipment. Individual choices clearly do matter.

If the overwhelming majority of people in a country were determined to end their consumption of fossil fuels, then the combination of their market decisions and their democratic decisions would deliver such an outcome. One country in the world will be the first to be powered fully by renewable energy – we just don't yet know which. Needless to say, there will be groups both inside and outside any country considering such a shift that will work hard to prevent it – the owners of petrol stations, for example – if only to stop a domino effect in other countries. But the potential for such a domino effect is perhaps one of the best reasons to try to achieve bold change at a small scale. In matters of democracy as well as in product design, imitation is often the sincerest form of flattery. And it is much harder to keep insisting that something is impossible when it is already happening somewhere else in the world.

As China has shown over the past decade, if a country wants to invest heavily in renewable energy and reduce its reliance on fossil fuels, the technology that will enable it to do so is readily available. China's pursuit of rapid reductions in fossil-fuel use is delivering significant health and political benefits, as well as the expected economic benefits: the capacity to export low-emission technologies to the world.

The United States spent a small fortune to put a man on the moon because its leaders and people wanted to. The French have subsidised the production and distribution of locally produced food because they wanted to. The United Kingdom is about to spend £20 billion on subsidies to ensure the Hinkley Point C nuclear power station is built ... presumably because the population can think of no better use for the money.

WE CAN DO ANYTHING (BUT NOT EVERYTHING)

How can one individual reshape the global economy? It's a fair question, but no one would ask if a single brick could reshape the Great Wall. Just as the more bricks you can place the more influence you will have on the shape of what is being built, the more people who share your goals the greater the impact you will collectively have on the shape of the economy.

As consumers, every time we spend a dollar we send a signal about the things we want more of and the things we want less of. As employees, every time we take a pay rise that is offered rather than request more holidays or a four-day week, we shift the distribution of work and income. And as citizens, every time we cast a vote we send a signal about what shape we want our economy to be – the things we want government to provide more of and the things we want them to provide less of. We can't always get what we want, but if our preferences are widely held, we should have no trouble getting what we need.

That said, not all citizens have the same number of dollars with which to 'vote' for the things they want. A person who earns $1 million a year has fifty times the influence on what the market will or won't produce than someone who earns $20,000 a year. Put simply, the distribution of income has a major impact on the 'will of the market' – which is why middle-class households throw out so much food while low-income earners often go hungry, and why some private schools have polo fields while some government schools can't afford chemicals for chemistry experiments. In the democratic domain some people obviously have more influence than others. For example, while some may argue that the appointment of former ExxonMobil CEO Rex Tillerson as the US Secretary of State does much to undermine the argument that all individuals are equal, in fact concern about how he might use his role is proof that individuals, and elections, can and do make a difference.

Similarly, when four-fifths of rich people (making more than $150,000) vote in US presidential elections but less than half of those making less than $10,000 do, it should not surprise us that governments focus on cutting the taxes paid by the rich rather than boosting the services on which low-income earners rely.[36] Like the shape of the global economy, the shape of a government's legislative agenda is influenced by the net effect of the pressures placed on it. When low-income earners don't vote, it is easier for politicians to deliver legislative outcomes for the high-income earners who do.

So what's a girl to do if she is keen to change the world as fast as possible? Shift her consumption patterns? Nag her parents to do likewise? Lobby a politician? Shift her vote? Organise a protest? Get her friends to vote? Run for office?

Why not do all of these things? While being strategic means different things in different contexts, it would be dangerous to mistake being focused for being strategic. History suggests that changing the world involves quite a few moving parts. No matter how important one element of a strategy may seem, it is unlikely to be the only thing that needs to happen to ensure large, rapid and lasting change at multiple levels of government in multiple countries.

While being focused is an important part of getting things done, so too is broadening your agenda to allow you to work with unlikely allies. Focusing on the priorities of your supporters is important to keep a movement together, but focusing on things that are important to your opponents can help you to divide and conquer. Changing behaviour one person at a time can be effective, and slow. Changing the law to change everyone's behaviour can be fast, but sometimes ineffective. So what is the right strategy? History also suggests that there is no such thing. Nokia's market power was not enough to protect its market share from the arrival of smartphones, but the coal industry's market power still protects it from the threat of renewables, in some countries at least. The public health lobby succeeded in removing lead from petrol in most countries, but it has been unable to prevent the sale of cars capable of driving at three times the legal maximum.

The ability to pick your battles, motivate your base, attract allies, communicate your message and drive the implementation of change that is actually effective is not evenly distributed across individuals, organisations and issues. Neither are the funds available to wage such campaigns. Given the wide range of factors that weigh on the political process it is impossible to predict which individuals, and which ideas, will drive change in the coming decades and which will try, and fail, despite their best efforts.

So if you want to reshape your local or national economy, would it be more strategic for you to focus on changing individual attitudes, cultural attitudes, government funding, legislative change or foreign policy? That is, what is the right way to go about changing the world? The point is that, as with the question that opened this book – Should we hurt the poor or hurt the environment? – this is not the right thing to ask.

More interesting questions for budding local organisers and global strategists are: What can I do at the personal or community level to help drive change at the national or global level? And what can we do at the national or global level to help drive change at the personal level?

NO ONE IS IN CHARGE OF THE FUTURE, BUT EVERYONE HAS A SAY IN HOW QUICKLY WE LEAVE THE PAST BEHIND

People, not 'the economy', will decide whether the new robots we invent will be used to clear landmines in Afghanistan or clear tables in your local restaurant.

The fear that robots will destroy human jobs is neither new nor ill-founded. They have in the past and they will in the future. The question is not whether labour-saving technologies will be developed and rolled out in the coming decades, but how the benefits of such change will be distributed.

Fear of the future and fear of unemployment make sense. But the belief that if we harm the environment enough, the economy will look after us in the future is irrational. The future will take shape in response to the largest pressures placed upon it. The first seventy years of the twentieth century showed that a motivated and demanding populace can drive major reforms in how work is organised, how income is distributed and how the environment is protected. The last forty years have shown that the course of history is not inevitable. No one can say what the next forty years hold, but history tells us that the coming decades, like all others, will be shaped by those who combine strategy with energy.

Kumi Naidoo

It is not easy to get to the tiny Pacific island nation of Kiribati; there is only one flight in and out each week. But my trip there in 2015 was worth it on so many levels. Not only are its people as good-humoured as they are generous, but the climate and the island landscape are, for me, near perfect.

But as the lowest-lying nation on earth, climate change does not just threaten to harm Kiribati, it threatens to submerge it completely. Unless we rapidly and dramatically reduce greenhouse-gas emissions, the nation of Kiribati and its population of 116,000 may go down in history as the first country to be wiped from the map as a result of the actions of other countries.

That's why I went there.

In the lead-up to that year's climate talks in Paris I went to talk to the then president of Kiribati, Anote Tong, about the need for bold leadership and the kind of campaign that simultaneously highlighted the enormity and the simplicity of the transition the world needs to make if countries like Kiribati are to have a future.

Soon after our meeting President Tong wrote a letter to all world leaders asking them to support his call for a global moratorium on building new coalmines. He did not call for all of the existing coalmines to shut down. He simply asked that other countries join him in agreeing that a world determined to reduce greenhouse-gas emissions was a world that needed fewer coalmines, not more.

The economist Sir Nicholas Stern was quick to support President Tong's call, as were climate scientists such as James Hansen and groups such as Greenpeace International, which I then led. But to date only thirteen other national leaders have been brave enough to call on countries such as Australia to stop building more of the coalmines that will cause more of the climate change that nations have agreed to prevent.

It is one thing for national leaders to agree in principle that we need to reduce greenhouse-gas emissions. To turn words into deeds those same leaders need to start doing more of the things that will reduce greenhouse-gas emissions and stop doing the things that will increase those emissions.

If the world heeded President Tong's call to stop building new coalmines there would still be much to do to make the climate, and Kiribati, safe. There will be a last coalmine built in the world. But the global community has not yet been able to agree whether that mine has already been built, or is yet to be built. But while new mines continue to be proposed, subsidised and built, people will keep standing against them. In tackling climate change and in shifting politics, actions speak louder than words.

Kumi Naidoo is the chair of Africans Rising for Justice, Peace and Dignity and former executive director of Greenpeace International.

6

Keeping on Track: Performance Indicators for a Better Society

'Anyone who believes exponential growth can go on forever in a finite world is either a madman or an economist.'

Kenneth Boulding, former president of the American Economics Association

How can you tell if your country, or your planet, is heading in the right direction? As we saw in the last chapter, the most important function of a democracy is to decide what things we want our cities, states or countries to do more of or less of. But after we decide on the ends, and before we start debating the means, we have to have a conversation about how we will measure our progress. How can you tell if your community is going to hell in a handbasket or is on the brink of becoming a utopia?

People who want to lose weight, run a marathon, learn a new language or write a book usually set themselves some goals, and then measure their progress towards them. So how would a country that wanted to lighten the load it placed on the environment or improve the quality of life of its citizens assess its progress towards those goals? The reality, unfortunately, is that it is a lot easier to decide that you *want* to measure progress than it is to decide *how* you will measure progress.

For the past forty years or so the main indicator of national performance has been gross domestic product. Many on the Right define their political agenda as the pursuit of a strong economy, as defined by growth in GDP. Progressive groups, on the other hand, are often divided between those who see strong economic growth as the only way to create jobs and lift people out of poverty, and those who see the pursuit of zero economic growth, or a 'steady-state economy', as the only path to environmental sustainability.

The inventors of GDP would be devastated to learn that their indicator of the amount of stuff that gets bought and sold each year has become the centre of our political galaxy, the thing around which far more important economic and democratic ideas now orbit. Although we run a risk that this chapter might be sucked into the political black hole that is the debate over whether GDP growth is good or bad, it is important to describe what GDP actually is, and is not, so that, with luck and determination, we can begin to escape its gravitational pull and move into a more interesting and fruitful space, where we can consider the significant policy and political trade-offs that always have to be resolved in a democracy.

WHAT IS GDP, AND WHAT ISN'T?

As we saw in Chapter 1, gross domestic product is a statistical estimate of the value of all of the goods and services (that is, all the stuff) that a country has produced in a particular time period. 'Economic growth' simply refers to the change in the size of GDP between one time period and the next. So if you hear someone say, 'The economy grew by 3 per cent last year,' what they really should have said was: 'According to the national statistics office, the estimated size of GDP was 3 per cent larger than last year's estimated size of GDP.'

Regardless of your politics or your goals for your country it is actually quite handy to know what the GDP is and whether it is shrinking or growing. Tracking progress and making good decisions requires information, and the national accounts on which GDP is based are jam-packed with useful information. But that doesn't mean it contains all the information we need.

So the problem isn't that we measure GDP. The problem is the way that GDP is used in political debate. Collecting data on production, consumption and investment is a great idea, but determining the success of a country by reference to GDP is like judging the success of your kid's birthday party by measuring how much you spent on the catering.

Few people work on the assumption that the more that is spent on something, the more successful it is. Indeed, it is absurd to conclude that the more economic activity there is, the more efficient the economy is becoming. But that is exactly the logic behind a belief that if GDP is growing, things must be improving. By that logic, if we all went and smashed our neighbour's windows, and then all paid a glazier to fix our own, we could make the economy stronger. The same would be true of causing climate change and then spending a fortune trying to protect ourselves from its consequences.

GDP is estimated by adding up the value of all the 'final goods and services' produced in an economy. It includes not just the value of the food we eat, but the food we throw in the bin. It includes the value of the landmines we produce, the value of the prisons we build and the value of cleaning up oil spills. Because it incorporates everything we spend money on, and ignores the value of housework, volunteers and the services the natural environment gives us for free, GDP is in no meaningful sense a measure of progress, as its inventors were eager to highlight; it is nothing more than a partial indicator of activity.

Here are a few things to keep in mind if you ever find yourself considering whether GDP is a good indicator of a country's wellbeing:

- When a farmer produces carrots and sells them to a shop and then the shop sells them to you, the value of the carrots is included in GDP. If you grow carrots in your own backyard and eat them, this is not included in GDP.

- When a farmer produces carrots and sells them to a shop and then the shop sells them to you, the value of the carrots is included in GDP. If the farmer trades a crate of carrots for a crate of eggs from the farmer next door, neither the eggs nor the carrots are included in GDP. (While they were 'produced', there is no paper trail for such bartering, so the statisticians can't measure it accurately.)

- When a farmer produces carrots and sells them to a shop and then the shop sells them to you, the value of the carrots is included in GDP. If you throw the carrots in the garbage bin, then the cost of collecting and disposing of the carrots will further add to GDP.

- When a farmer uses pesticide to produce carrots, and the pesticide runs off into a river and kills a large number of fish, the cost of the pesticide, which is passed on to consumers, is included in GDP. If the fish would otherwise have been caught and sold, then the death of the fish will lead to a reduction in GDP. But if not, their death has no effect on GDP. Any money spent trying to keep the pesticide out of the water supply would, however, increase GDP further.

As we have seen, Simon Kuznets, one of the inventors of GDP, was fully aware of its limitations as a measure. In 1962 he said:

The welfare of a nation can scarcely be inferred from a measure of national income. If the GDP is up, why is America down? Distinctions must be kept in mind between quantity and quality of growth, between costs and returns, and between the short and long run. Goals for more growth should specify more growth of what and for what.[37]

GDP DOESN'T MISLEAD – PEOPLE DO

If you want to know how much stuff was produced and sold in your country last year, then GDP is your go-to number. But if you want to know what is happening to employment in the retail sector, then GDP isn't that useful because it doesn't distinguish between sales of shoes made in shoe stores and sales of shoes online. Given that shoe stores employ a lot more people than online retailers, the shift to online shopping means there is no longer a stable link between shoe sales and jobs for shoe salespeople. In turn, it is no longer safe to assume that if we all buy a lot of stuff, we will create a lot of jobs. The shape of our economies is changing, and some of it is bad news for retail workers.

The ever-changing shape of the economy is one of the main reasons that it makes little sense to pursue GDP as a national goal. Consider the following:

- It is possible to have rapid economic growth without rapid employment growth when the parts of the economy that don't need a lot of workers (such as online retail, mining and financial services) are doing most of the growing.

- It is possible to have rapid economic growth while the incomes of low- and middle-income earners fall – as long as the incomes of the rich rise even faster; this is because GDP measures total production and says nothing about distribution.

- It is possible to have rapid economic growth and rapid destruction of natural resources; this is because the sale price of commodities such as coal, oil and wood are included in GDP, but the reduction in value of the stock of natural resources is not.

The economists and statisticians employed to estimate GDP today are fully aware of these and many more limitations. The bottom line is that it is not GDP that is at fault; the problem is its use and abuse by those who should know better. If you want an indication of whether a country is heading in the right direction, you need to consider other things.

GROWTH IS GOOD... SOMETIMES

When you're talking about the development of a child, the expansion of the renewable energy industry or the proportion of people who have access to clean drinking water, growth is most likely to be good. But growth is a process, not a universal goal. It's not whether or not growth is occurring that matters, but whether the growth of an activity or industry helps or hinders achieving your actual goals. Rapid weight growth in an infant, for example, is usually a sign of good health, but in an adult it is probably not.

Despite the economic, social and rhetorical benefits of the pursuit of growth (the pursuit of decline being a far less attractive proposition for most), many on the progressive side of politics are quick to state their opposition to, or at least their concern with, economic growth. However, being a critic of growth creates not only political difficulties but also policy problems that could be easily avoided.

Consider the following examples. Many in the environmental movement say they want to slow or even stop economic growth, but they simultaneously say they want hundreds of billions of dollars invested in renewable energy to rapidly reduce greenhouse-gas emissions. Such investment, if it were to occur, would likely stimulate economic growth. Is that good or bad? Similarly, many advocates for economic justice want big pay rises for low-income workers and a massive increase in funding for schools, hospitals and aged-care facilities. Such spending would almost certainly lead to an increase in economic growth. Would that be good or bad?

A phoney debate has raged for decades about whether economic growth is good or bad, and while this has kept both sides busy, it has come at the expense of a far more important debate: what *kind* of economic growth is needed to get society and the natural environment into the shape we want it in?

Middle-class people living in developed countries would do well to admit that two centuries of economic growth has produced a substantial increase in human life expectancy and a significant improvement in the physical standard of living for the majority of the population. The fact that it has also driven high rates of biodiversity loss around the world and a rapid reduction in the amount of open space per person, and done little to address the disadvantage of many of the most vulnerable groups in the community (especially segments of Indigenous communities) is, again, a reflection of the shape of economic growth, not proof that the rate of economic growth has been too slow – or too fast.

Citizens of developed countries today live in the most materially affluent societies the world has ever known. Middle-class people in countries such as Australia, Canada or the USA have access to better food, better health care, better transport and have far longer life expectancies than even pharaohs and emperors of distant eras could have imagined. Social, technological and economic change has delivered enormous benefits, but those benefits can no more be measured by the volume of stuff that is produced than a movie can be judged by how long it is.

MY FLAWED INDICATOR OF PROGRESS IS BETTER THAN YOURS

Agents of change need a clear vision. New indicators (or making better use of the old indicators) will help, but just as a compass can tell you which way you are pointing but not which way to go, no indicator of 'progress' or 'well-being' can tell a democracy what it should have more of and what it should be willing to give up to achieve it.

As GDP approaches its hundredth birthday it is beginning to show significant signs of age. As the 'P' in GDP makes clear, it is focused on production, but a growing proportion of economic activity in developed countries has very little to do with production in the sense that economists in the 1940s understood it. Furthermore, while the boundary between market production (which is included in GDP) and household production (which is not) has always been a problem, this is now becoming a central concern for economists and policy-makers. As the *Economist* magazine has observed:

> In a world where houses are Airbnb hotels and
> private cars are Uber taxis, where a free software
> upgrade renews old computers, and Facebook and

YouTube bring hours of daily entertainment to
hundreds of millions at no price at all, many suspect
GDP is becoming an ever more misleading measure.

If companies such as Facebook and Google decide they
want their contribution to society to be recognised, they
may become some of the most influential advocates for
reforming GDP and developing new indicators of progress
the world has ever seen.

The glaring problems with GDP have led to the creation of a wide range of alternative indicators, including
the Genuine Progress Indicator, the Index of Social and
Economic Wellbeing, the Human Development Index
and the Sustainable Development Goals. Some of these
measures start with GDP and adjust it for the things their
authors believe should be included or excluded. The other
common approach is to develop a broad scorecard of
indicators for a wide range of social and environmental
variables. But while all such efforts perform the valuable
function of broadening the range of information available
to voters and decision-makers, none is widely used, and
none is a substitute for the democratic question: What do
we want more of?

The uncomfortable truth for those who see GDP as bad
is that no single indicator – of GDP, wellbeing, progress,
sustainability or happiness – is ever likely to be widely recognised as good. In turn, no new indicator, no matter how

worthy or how superior to GDP it might be, is ever likely to be widely accepted by tens or hundreds of millions of people. Significantly, the decisions about what to include in GDP – and what to leave out – were never voted on by the public or politicians. Nor was how health and education services should be 'valued'. GDP was invented behind closed doors and has grown to be used in precisely the ways its inventors feared. The idea that any new alternative to GDP can be agreed to by a parliament and then embraced around the world is as absurd as the current assumption by those who construct the national accounts that Wikipedia provides no benefit to the economy and that making landmines does.

But despite the political difficulty – dare I say impossibility? – of creating a new indicator that is not just clearly superior to GDP but can be widely accepted by groups as diverse as arms manufacturers and charities, there is a steady stream of efforts to develop the 'one true indicator' of progress. Just as GDP gives many politicians and business leaders some simplicity and certainty, so too, it seems, many would-be reformers have invested their hopes in the development of happiness or sustainable wellbeing measures. If we had such measures, the argument goes, we would be able to ensure that the country was on track towards happiness or wellbeing. Such indicators, it is suggested, can ensure that decisions are made in the 'true national interest'.

If only. Those on the progressive side of politics are often fierce critics of the idea that it is possible to develop a simple numerical indicator of the performance of a school-teacher, the quality of education provided by a school or even the benefits to the economy of training students in the arts or philosophy. But, strangely, many of those who are adamant that their own job or industry defies measurement by 'simplistic indicators' seem to believe that if we could somehow measure the value of volunteer effort, investments in crime prevention and improvements in air quality, we could then combine them in some way and – hey presto! – we would know whether our country was going in the right direction or not. Imagine getting the National Rifle Association and the health profession to agree on whether both the sale of guns and the cost of treating gunshot wounds should be included in a new measure of progress. Or imagine getting fundamentalist Christians and medical professionals to agree on whether the cost of providing abortions adds to or detracts from national wellbeing.

IT'S NEVER BEEN 'ALL ABOUT THE ECONOMY'

There is no evidence to support the view that conservative governments, or any governments, are singularly obsessed with maximising GDP growth. If they were, these governments would invest a lot more money in early childhood education, provide a lot more support to help parents (usually women) re-enter the workforce after they have children, spend a lot more money on crime prevention and a lot more money on preventative health. Although all of these simple policies have been shown to provide large long-term economic benefits, conservative governments often prefer to cut spending in these areas in the name of reducing the size of the 'inefficient' public sector.

Given a choice between cutting public-sector programs or spending more money on public-sector projects that increase the size of the economy, most conservatives would opt for the cuts. While progressives often accuse conservatives of being obsessed with the economy, such criticism unduly flatters those conservatives.

Consider the following. The 'war on drugs' has been raging for decades, with no sign of victory in sight. Not only is the cost of such a war high in financial terms, the human cost of criminalising common cultural behaviours is also devastating for individuals and communities. Further, the benefits to individuals, government budgets and the economy more generally of harm minimisation approaches to illicit drug use have been shown to be substantial. Yet despite the costs to the budget and the economy, many conservatives insist on a tough-on-crime approach for the simple reason that they are not really obsessed by GDP. They just like sounding tough on crime. It's cultural.

As we've seen, the decisions to put a man on the moon, end slavery, declare war, grant women the vote, end apartheid, build nuclear weapons, vote for Brexit or allow the sale of automatic weapons have nothing to do with maximising the rate of GDP growth. While there is no doubt that politicians in many countries are keen to see the rapid growth of the parts of the economy that they like, it is simply not the case that maximising economic growth lies at the heart of all government decisions in any country.

Ironically, while many progressives think that economists and conservative politicians are always singularly obsessed with maximising the rate of GDP growth, in reality even the most avowedly free-market economists think that economic growth is sometimes unsustainably high. As high rates of GDP growth can cause inflation, and inflation can undermine the value of bonds and other financial assets, economists often call on governments to rein in the rate of economic growth. Needless to say, when environmentalists call on governments to rein in economic growth to preserve the value of natural assets, they are far less likely to be taken seriously.

While GDP is a widely used summary indicator, it is simply not true to suggest that government policy is always directed towards its growth. In addition to the determination to neglect public investment as described above, governments around the world often seek to lower their country's rate of growth to reduce inflation, imports and foreign borrowing. Put simply, while GDP growth is often used to justify policies, in reality elected politicians and central bank staffers are always making judgement calls about what the 'right' thing to do is. Using econobabble about the need to 'reduce liquidity in order to lower inflationary expectations to ensure that GDP remains on its full employment growth path' is just a way to conceal the implications of the judgement calls about what is 'good for the economy' that are being made on our behalf all the time.

CHOOSING THE BEST CAR IN THE WORLD

Formula 1 racing cars are very fast, but they can't carry passengers, can't go over speed bumps and fall apart in the smallest of collisions. They are loud, uncomfortable to sit in and have no room for luggage. Their fuel economy isn't great either.

Designing a car that can travel at 300 kilometres per hour is an incredible feat of engineering, but the skill required to build such a car cannot compensate for how useless it is for many of the activities that are really important to humans. It is next to worthless in all but the most artificial of environments.

So, when designing our economy, should we aim for top speed? Or safety? Or comfort? Or low emissions? The focus in public debate on maximising the economy's rate of growth has negated the possibility of a more nuanced, but more useful, debate about the kind of features a democracy might want from economic activity. Political and business leaders have for decades seemed determined to create an economy that is designed for speed rather than comfort or safety. Given a choice between increasing the top speed and safely transporting our children into the future, the choice seems clear: the faster, the better ...

Adolescents often believe that their driving skill can compensate for the high speeds at which some of them drive. Adolescents are also far more likely to crash. It is not just society that needs to grow up – it is also our policymakers. Bragging about how fast an economy is growing is like bragging about a car's top speed. The fact that the claims might be true doesn't make them important or meaningful, especially in a country with speed limits.

Economic growth, like a car's top speed, is an indicator of potential. Both provide a narrow but, for many, seductive indication of performance. But just as the decisions of a family man who returns from a car dealer with a fast, expensive and impractical sports car should be carefully scrutinised before anyone applauds, so too should the decisions of any politician whose only claim to fame is that they think they can make the economy go fast. Maybe they can – but the real questions are 'In what direction?' and 'At what risk?'

So which is the best car, then? Is it the one with the best fuel economy, the one with the most comfortable ride or the one that tells the neighbours how wealthy you are? The answer, of course, is that it depends on what you want the car to do. In every country, in every year, some automotive experts set out to determine the Car of the Year, but despite all the data they collect and the diversity of the judges they recruit, there is no consensus about which car is actually the best. Indeed, the vast majority of the car-buying public does not buy the 'best' car. They buy the one they think suits their needs.

New indicators of progress that draw on a wider range of information than GDP can play an important role in highlighting the limitations of GDP, but broad indicators that seek to place a cash value on human life, the natural environment and our sense of community are not a light on the hill to steer towards, but a mirage that often lures well-meaning reformers into an empty desert.

The purpose of elections is to set national goals and to select the policies that are best able to achieve those goals – in effect, they are a national fight about what kind of car we collectively need to move our country forward. Information can help exclude poor choices and highlight better ones, but ultimately the choice comes down to the direction we want to head in, our priorities, and the things we are willing to sacrifice to get what we want.

If you were trying to rebuild Europe after World War II, or you were trying to lift people in a poor region out of poverty, it is more likely that the faster the growth in economic activity, the better. Anyone today who is concerned with unemployment, investment in infrastructure and the capacity to shift to a low-carbon economy should be as interested in GDP as those responsible for post-war reconstruction in the 1950s. But 'interested in' doesn't mean 'obsessed by'.

Rather than simply dismissing GDP as a tool of destruction, those who seek to build a new economy need to use GDP like police use radar guns: to detect those parts of the economy that are going faster, or slower, than is socially desirable. Surely those who want to transition to a zero-carbon economy want to see rapid growth in investment in renewable energy and public transport? Surely those who want to improve aged care want to see rapid growth in the relevant parts of the construction industry? GDP figures will give them a straighter answer than a politician ever will about what *is* really happening. But GDP figures can never tell us what *should* be happening.

MEASURING WHAT MATTERS

During World War II, GDP was specifically designed to help monitor the level of production of guns, tanks and battleships. Yet many citizens (outside the United States at least) might argue that sales of guns today are linked to a decline in wellbeing, not an increase. That is, while keeping track of the value of transactions is an economic issue, evaluating what we need more of and what we need less of is a democratic issue.

In large and diverse populations, it is much easier to measure progress towards a goal than it is to achieve consensus about which goals should be pursued. Similarly, it is much easier to measure the number of children who can read when they leave school than it is to agree whether having another literate child is more or less important than the protection of an endangered species or the preservation of an endangered Indigenous language.

If children's literacy, species protection and the preservation of Indigenous cultures seem like strange things to compare, then you can see the problem with any effort to develop the one true indicator of national progress. Those who would replace GDP with a better indicator must collect data on those and hundreds or thousands of things that matter to them but are excluded from GDP and, having collected all that information, combine it into a single indicator of national progress, decline or stasis. And in combining all the things that matter, they must make assumptions about what number of literate children outweighs the impact of a species becoming extinct. Unless a common unit of measure for education, biodiversity and Indigenous-language usage can be found, it is impossible to combine such issues into a summary indicator.

A simpler and more transparent approach would be to collect, compile and publish a wide range of raw data on the diverse range of issues that matter to people, and then to discuss them regularly, publicly and in the context that while rich countries cannot do *everything* that they want, they can do *anything* they want.

Today, of course, while GDP gets most of the headlines, data on inflation, unemployment, wage growth, trade balances and public debt are all part of a very human, very flexible and very subjective decision-making process relating to changes in interest rates and budgetary policy. Indeed, a key indicator used by those setting monetary and fiscal policy is surveys of business confidence and consumer sentiment, both of which are subjective attempts to gauge how managers and consumers are feeling.

Those who want to cure affluenza do not need to develop the one true indicator of progress. They need only ensure that voters, and those politicians who want the support of voters, are clear about the performance of the things that matter to them. They must understand that if politicians want to spend more money on key problems, they can – if they want to. Arguing that more resources can't be devoted to health, education or renewable energy because we must grow our GDP is not a valid reason for inaction: it is simply an excuse.

IT'S TIME TO GROW UP, NOT OUT

Of course, 'growth' doesn't only refer to size: it can also refer to maturity. 'Growing up' means much more than getting taller.

Keynes once wrote: 'The day is not far off when the economic problem will take the back seat where it belongs, and the arena of the heart and the head will be occupied or reoccupied, by our real problems of life and of human relations, of creation and behaviour and religion.' While he might have got the timing wrong, the significance of his observation stands. At some point we will have enough stuff that we won't have to worry so much about stuff. The question isn't if, but when. When will national leaders feel confident enough about the size of their economy that they can start focusing on the way their society treats its people? When will we sate our hunger for more stuff and start to put something aside for our children? When will we be rich enough as a society that we can afford to be generous to our neighbours?

This simple truth has been observed not just by the economists who gave us GDP, but also by philosophers, artists and politicians. 'It is not enough to be busy,' said Henry David Thoreau. 'So are the ants. The question is: What are we busy about?'

Marilyn Waring

All of the women in my family were fabulous housekeepers and beautiful gardeners. They made gardens wherever they went. These women worked really hard and didn't get a cent but it didn't enter my mind to think they weren't working. But in my twenties I came to realise that the United Nations System of National Accounts, the international rules for measuring GDP, literally defined household work, most of which is done by women, as worthless. It was a source of real anger for me. I was outraged.

When I wrote *Counting for Nothing* in 1988 I thought it was really important to confront the public, politicians and the economics profession with the shortcomings of GDP and the way it ignored the work of women and the value of the services produced by the natural environment. I was surprised at how much interest there was in the issues it raised, and I was proud of the way that so many countries, and the UN itself, took up the challenge of collecting a wider range of data and presenting it in a wider context.

But the importance of counting is one of the major things that I've changed my mind about. When I was writing that book I had just stepped out of the New Zealand parliament. When you are in parliament you want data, you want numbers. But it is easy to confuse having precise numbers with having a clear picture of what's going on. I have moved on from that way of thinking.

I now think estimating the value of the environment and of unpaid work is a pretty stupid thing to do. The dollar values that we use for air pollution or water pollution or caring for a baby can end up attracting more attention than the need for clean air or healthy babies and, in turn, putting dollar values on such things can make it easier for decision-makers to lose track of what is really important. These are abstracted indicators. They do not tell you, for example, the density of harmful particulate matter and what those particles do to a child's lung, which is what a decision-maker needs to consider. We can't really put a dollar value on the benefit of a child being able to breathe easily.

I began to do more work around broad measures of wellbeing and then got impatient with that too, because everybody was trying to expand GDP with a load of other indicators that were inevitably decided by some form of central committee. And the things that got added in tended to be things there was already some old data for, as opposed to the new things you thought should be measured.

It's crucial to realise how important is the decision about which things to include in a measure of wellbeing, and which things to leave out. It's central to the final results – but who gets to decide what's in and out? The things that 'matter' depend on your gender, age, culture and even on what we have come to expect will be measured. Unfortunately I have come to believe that homogenised indicators of national wellbeing are barren for policy-making as well.

That said, I do think that measuring GDP is better than nothing, and I think that collecting and reporting broader indicators of wellbeing is better than just measuring GDP. I think some researchers and some governments have used data on household production and other non-market services well, but I don't think it is possible, or desirable, to develop the 'uber-indicator' that can tell elected representatives what to do. Ultimately decisions and trade-offs have to be made by informed and well-intentioned parliamentarians who have been elected by well-informed citizens.

Professor Marilyn Waring is an economist, feminist and former member of the New Zealand parliament whose work on GDP is widely credited with changing the way the UN measured GDP and understood wellbeing.

7

There Are Many Alternatives

Deciding what you want your country to do more of is one thing; knowing how to track progress towards it is another thing entirely. But actually making it happen? Driving social change, even when opposed by powerful people? That's crazy talk. The market won't allow it. The system can't be changed. Don't you know there is no alternative?

Except, of course, there are countless alternatives. And many of them are already working well in parts of the world. The future is already here; it just hasn't been widely copied yet.

Canberra, Australia's capital city, will operate on 100 per cent renewable energy by 2020. Half of Copenhagen's commuters ride their bikes to work, and the city is now building a bike 'superhighway'. Towns in Canada, Australia, the United States and India have introduced a variety of bans and limitations on the sale of bottled water, plastic shopping bags and other products the world once lived without. Volunteers built (and continue to build) Wikipedia, and in doing so made information freely available to billions of people and saved millions of tonnes of paper that would once have filled bookshelves with out-of-date facts. Swedish workers have five weeks of paid holidays each year. Credit unions and co-operatives have, for more than a century, provided all of the services of global banks, usually at lower prices – and with any surplus invested in their communities. Cuba has a poor economy and a great health system.

You don't need permission, or global consensus, to change the world. Indeed, changing the world doesn't even require co-ordinated global action. There was, for example, no United Nations resolution to roll out smartphones across the world, to move from horses to cars, or to make QWERTY keyboards the norm. While global agreements to encourage things, or to ban things, play an important role in shifting norms, cultures and expectations, they don't always work. The fact that there is an international ban on whaling has not stopped the Japanese from whaling, and the fact that there is a global non-proliferation treaty on nuclear weapons has not stopped a number of countries from seeking or developing them. Most international agreements, by design, lack enforcement mechanisms. Their main strength is that they can help to change culture – but international agreements are by no means the only way to do so.

UNTHINKABLE THOUGHTS

The US health system is based on private funding, while in the United Kingdom it is almost entirely publicly funded. In Australia there's a bit of both, but the system is much closer to the UK's than the US's. The United Kingdom instituted its National Health Service in 1948; Australia's publicly funded Medicare system was introduced in 1984. In each case, five years earlier a public health system was inconceivable. While Obamacare in the United States is not a publicly funded health model, it did help millions of low-income earners afford private health insurance. Its repeal by President Trump in early 2017 was considered inevitable – right up until the Republicans in Congress failed to do so.

History suggests that no one can predict what in the future will stop seeming a totally crazy idea. Certainly the notions that the United Kingdom would vote to leave the European Union, that a US president would be elected on a promise to remove the country from the North American Free Trade Agreement, or that bottled water might outsell Coca-Cola were unthinkable only a decade ago. But all have come to pass.

During the last thirty years, the International Monetary Fund, the World Bank and many Western governments told billions of people that free markets were good, that protecting industries was bad, and that bailing out failing companies was an ineffective way to help workers, consumers or the economy as a whole. Until, that is, the biggest banks in the world needed a bailout. Then, of course, voters learned that there were alternatives. Much of the so-called populism that has emerged around the world in recent years – movements that support subsidies and trade barriers – has been a direct reaction to the obvious willingness and ability of governments to bail out the banks that nearly failed in the global financial crisis. If we can support the banks, billions of people realised, why can't we support local manufacturing? It's a fair question, and one for which the spokespeople for the 'There Is No Alternative' bloc – sometimes known as TINA – have absolutely no answer.

Intriguingly, not all countries bailed out their failing banks after the global financial crisis. Iceland's banks, like those in the United Kingdom, the United States and elsewhere, made lots of bad loans to lots of people who had no real prospect of repaying them. And like in most other countries, the owners of Iceland's banks argued that if they weren't bailed out by taxpayers, the whole economy would collapse. But unlike in most other countries, Iceland's governments ignored these pleas. While the bank's shareholders lost a lot of money, Iceland's economy is still with us. Indeed, because Iceland's taxpayers didn't spend billions bailing out their nation's banks, Iceland's economy recovered from the global financial crisis more quickly than most.

The strongest and most stable era of economic growth in developed economies occurred after World War II. Then, there were virtually no free-trade agreements between nations, the finance sector accounted for a tiny proportion of national economies, and real wages grew steadily for low- and middle-income earners. Corporate tax rates were high by today's standards, and governments provided a wide range of services directly to citizens.

The idea that there is no alternative to free-trade agreements that undermine national regulatory standards, to corporate tax cuts and to lower wages is clearly contradicted by the recorded history of every developed country. Similarly, the fact that the most prosperous countries in the world have some of the largest public sectors, some of the highest tax rates and some of the highest wages in the world tends to confirm not just the existence of alternatives, but their success.

WHAT'S ON THE POLICY MENU? AND WHO'S ORDERING?

'First they ignore you, then they laugh at you, then they fight you, then you win.'

Mahatma Gandhi

Australians are unique in their willingness to eat both the animals that appear on the national coat of arms. This hasn't been the case for very long, however. While

Indigenous Australians had always eaten kangaroo and emu, most immigrants to Australia chose to stay away from the native fauna, preferring domesticated cattle, sheep, pigs and chicken as sources of animal protein. But cultures change all the time.

Some visitors to Australia are shocked to see kangaroo on restaurant menus, while others go out of their way to taste it. From time to time consumers in various countries embrace the novelty and supposed health benefits of kangaroo meat (which is high in protein but low in fat), while others protest what they perceive as the cruelty of hunting and butchering wild animals for human consumption.

Both eating meat and choosing which meats are acceptable to eat are entirely cultural decisions. Some cultures love bacon; others see the pig as a filthy animal. Some cultures eat dogs and cats; others do not. Certain cultures are strongly vegetarian; in some, people don't consume much meat due to the fact that, without refrigeration, fresh meat is difficult and expensive to come by.

Every few years, a scientist looking for publicity will release research suggesting that world hunger can be addressed if more people were willing to eat maggots, crickets and cockroaches. But while most of us recoil in horror at the thought of eating insect protein, anyone who thinks bugs are gross should have a close look at a prawn or a lobster before it's cooked. There's a good reason prawns are sometimes called the cockroaches of the sea.

Whether it is a restaurant menu or tax rates, culture plays the dominant role in shaping not just the choices that we make but also, and more importantly, the choices that we are offered. This is as true for individuals shopping for groceries as it is for politicians shopping for ideas.

The length of the menu of policy ideas that politicians feel they can draw from is heavily influenced by the temper of the times. The passage of the Patriot Act in the aftermath of the horrific events of September 11, 2001, is a good example. Before the attacks, the idea of giving police unfettered powers to surveil citizens would have seemed more than a little radical, but a month after the attacks the US Senate voted by a margin of 98 to 1 in favour of a bill that did exactly that. An extreme event shifted the way a culture viewed surveillance: less emphasis was placed on citizens' privacy and more on their need for security. The fact that every country strikes a different balance when trading off privacy against security is proof that there is no right answer here. Not only do different countries with different cultures strike different balances, but as cultures change within countries, so too do citizens' perceptions of the right balance change over time.

The concept of the 'Overton window' is sometimes used to describe the range of ideas deemed to be politically acceptable in a particular time and place. According to Joseph P. Overton, after whom the effect is named, only ideas that are considered politically acceptable in the current climate of public opinion can be recommended by a politician if he or she wants to gain or retain public office. While the position of the Overton window can be shifted gradually through public debate or rapidly through significant events (such as the September 11 terrorist attacks) to propose an idea that is outside of the current Overton window is to reveal yourself as radical and, more importantly, unelectable. Expanding on Gandhi's observation, the political commentator Joshua Trevino spelt out the path an idea follows as it moves from outside the Overton window to its centre as:

1. Unthinkable
2. Radical
3. Acceptable
4. Sensible
5. Popular
6. Policy

It was once unthinkable for politicians to propose that black people or women might have the vote. It is currently radical to suggest that fifteen-year-olds should vote, and unthinkable to suggest that 99-year-olds should not. Women in Saudi Arabia first cast their votes in 2015. In Australia it is radical to propose that people should be able to buy machine guns and armour-piercing bullets. In the United States it is unthinkable – at least, for those seeking to hold public office – to suggest that all private gun ownership be banned. The majority of Australians support exactly such a position. Culture drives policy.

When mobile phones first came into common use, it was unheard of for someone to maintain a phone conversation while engaging with shop assistants. When email first came into common use you could opt to receive correspondence electronically; now many firms charge extra, or simply refuse, to send information by 'snail mail'. Culture shapes expectations.

Culture doesn't change like the seasons; it is changed by the actions of people within it. In turn, when people say that there is no alternative to the current health system – or no alternative to the way that cities are designed around cars, or no alternative to the way that income generated through profits is taxed at lower rates than income generated through working all day – what they really mean is: 'I like things the way they are.'

Many people believe that the United States could never introduce effective regulation of large corporations, make share-owners pay more tax, or invest any extra tax revenue in high-quality health, education and infrastructure services. Perhaps they don't understand that things were not always this way and that the US was once far more 'progressive' than Europe. As Don Watson observes:

the New Deal ... made the US more socially progressive than any country in Europe. For half a century after Roosevelt's election, tax on incomes over a million dollars averaged 82 per cent. US estate taxes of 70–80 per cent were twice those in Germany and France. Wisconsin was a state as progressive as any in the world, and the South aside, the US did not lag so far behind. Yet by the mid-1980s it had been decided that these rates and a federal minimum wage which had co-existed with the most sustained era of prosperity and social mobility in US history were an unbearable burden on free enterprise and the American way.[38]

In 1910 it was unthinkable that a government would seek to break up J.D. Rockefeller's company Standard Oil, at the time the most profitable firm in the world. But the temper of the times changed, and after a 1911 Supreme Court case ruled that Standard Oil should be broken up, by the beginning of World War I the unthinkable had become policy. The Overton window can open faster than those who profit from the status quo, and those who want change, often realise.

But the fact that the window can be flung open does not mean that it can't be slammed shut or, more likely, slip down quietly over time. The laws that reined in the 'robber barons' of the early twentieth century were steadily eroded and circumvented over the next eighty years, so that by the end of the century the scene was set for a repeat performance. It may seem unlikely that the United States is set to return to the culture, and the policies, that delivered the incredible period of economic growth and redistribution from 1945 to 1970, but unlikely doesn't mean impossible. It might be just another court case away. No wonder judicial appointments have become so political in the United States.

History is full of stories about how leaders such as Roosevelt, Gandhi and Churchill each changed their nation's culture, and in turn their nation, through force of will. So we know it can happen; we just can't be sure when it will happen next. But history is also full of more complicated stories, such as the centuries it took for women to get the vote, a project completed only recently and already in need of significant preventive maintenance. Similarly, the abolitionists fought for hundreds of years to end slavery; despite their obvious success in some countries, it is estimated that between 21 million and 46 million people, mainly women, are today held as slaves.

The world is full of alternative ways to structure our lives, our communities and our countries. We can learn from the past, learn from other countries or think up new ways of doing things ourselves. Collecting the evidence that a problem exists and that solutions can work is sometimes an important part of driving policy change, but there is no evidence to support the view held by many progressives that 'evidence-based' policy is a good way to drive change in a democracy. There is also no strong evidence that causing climate change is a good way to help create jobs and there is no strong evidence that corporate tax cuts are a good way to create jobs. But powerful voices not only hold these views strongly, they have also managed to turn them into policy.

Those who want to solve their community's problems, or the world's problems, should draw on the best evidence available to help them choose among existing alternatives or design new solutions. But those who want not just to imagine alternatives, but to drive them, should never believe that once they have presented the evidence for change, powerful interests who benefit from the status quo will simply step out of the way. As Michel Foucault observed, 'Where there is power, there is resistance.'

DO WE NEED TO SMASH CAPITALISM?

The term capitalism isn't very helpful anymore. Capitalist used to refer to someone whose income came from the capital they had accumulated. Workers got income from their work, and capitalists got income from their capital. Now the term capitalist is often embraced by people who work for a living but like the idea of free markets. But a lot of the biggest capitalists – that is, those who have the most capital – accumulated their wealth specifically because regulations have protected them from the competition that comes with free markets. Media barons are a case in point: their most valuable asset is a broadcasting licence that prevents new competitors from entering the market without first compensating the incumbents.

Not only is capitalism used in contradictory ways by different people, the idea of reforming or even smashing capitalism means different things to different people. When it comes to the goal of smashing capitalism, for example, should the small farmers selling their organic produce to the locals be destroyed first? Or the giant multinationals such as Tesla, which is disrupting the global oil and coal industry with its mass production of batteries? Maybe the artists selling their work direct to customers on eBay should be the first target? Or perhaps Facebook, which among other things allows community groups to organise far more quickly than ever before?

While there are plenty of reasons to think that in a hundred or a thousand years' time there might be economic systems that do not rely on the generation of private profit from privately owned property, there are also plenty of reasons to think that the path from the status quo to a fundamentally different culture might be more incremental (and hopefully more peaceful) than the kind of revolution that so many communists hoped was just around the corner.

The idea that capitalism can be tamed, and the profit motive directed towards the collective good, is long-standing but widely mocked in some circles. Since Engels in 1893 some communists have argued that it is naive to think you can simply knock the sharp edges of capitalism through 'reform'. Such incrementalism is often portrayed as false consciousness and its proponents accused of propping up the status quo by damping down revolutionary tendencies.

Maybe they're right. But whether people believe that the revolution is coming, the revolution will never come or the revolution is already happening every day, they should at least be able to agree that it is beneficial to help individuals, communities and countries understand the vast array of alternative forms of production and economic organisation that already exist around the world. Surely those who want to smash capitalism and those who want to reform it would both benefit in the short term from helping billions of people understand that we do not all owe our jobs, our happiness or our health to the big corporations that we hear so much about. There are alternatives.

Far more people play for local sporting teams than for the national sporting teams that dominate the sports coverage on the nightly news. Indeed, if you only relied on the national media, you could be forgiven for assuming that nobody played amateur sport. The same is true of small business. While far more people work in small business than in the big companies that dominate media coverage of the economy, you could be forgiven for thinking that nearly everyone owes their jobs to the handful of big companies that attract the vast majority of attention. But they don't.

BIG COMPANIES AREN'T THAT BIG A DEAL

Four of the five biggest companies on the US stock market didn't exist in 1975, and none of them was in the top ten even twenty years ago. In 2006 the three biggest companies in the world were ExxonMobil, General Electric and Gazprom. In 2016 the biggest three were Apple, Alphabet (the owner of Google) and Microsoft. ExxonMobil has grown rapidly in the last fifty years and is now the biggest oil company in the world, but it has shed half of its workforce over that time. Growth in the value of a company is in no way linked to growth in the number of people it employs.

The fact that there are big companies in the world doesn't mean that change is impossible, or even hard. In fact, big change is often driven by big companies. As we have seen, J.D. Rockefeller's Standard Oil grew so big at the beginning of the twentieth century that new laws had to be created to control the power he wielded. But the reason that Standard Oil grew so big so fast was that it was helping the world move through one of the biggest economic transitions it has ever seen: the transition from steam engines to internal-combustion engines.

The incredible growth in the use of smartphones, not just as a means for people to call each other but as a way to book hotels, buy groceries and find our way around cities, would not have occurred as rapidly as it has without Apple, a company that was nearly broke in 1997. In fact,

without Apple and the smartphone it is highly unlikely that
Uber, Google, Amazon and Facebook would have grown
so fast either.

Of course big companies can, and do, use their shareholders' and customers' money to shape both the culture
and the laws of the countries they operate in. ExxonMobil,
for example, has spent tens of millions of dollars funding
climate sceptics, in a deliberate attempt to undermine any
sense that we need to use less fossil fuels. Such manipula-
tion of culture is neither new nor confined to the fossil-fuel
industry. In addition to funding scientists to dispute the
health risks of smoking, the tobacco industry engaged in
a decades-long culture war to undermine the evidence of
the harm its products caused, while simultaneously working hard (and spending harder) to depict smoking as
something done by rugged individuals who were proud
of taking risks.

One of the clearest and longest-lasting efforts to
reshape culture was undertaken by the De Beers diamond company. After watching the demand for, and price
of, diamonds collapse during the Great Depression, De
Beers wrote to an advertising company, N.Y. Ayer & Sons,
asking whether 'the use of propaganda in various forms'
might increase demand for its product. Market research
confirmed that a large proportion of American women
saw diamonds as 'money down the drain'. Undeterred, the
advertising company set out to 'create a situation where

almost every person pledging marriage feels compelled to acquire a diamond engagement ring'. Needless to say, it worked.

But the fact that the owners of big companies have managed to bend culture and laws to suit their own interests does not mean that they always can, or indeed that they will always be able to. The very fact that large companies, churches, political parties and others set out to shape culture is, for others who wish to change the world, proof of the importance of actively doing so.

It is not as easy for individuals, small businesses or non-government organisations to shape culture as it can be for companies that stand to make billions of dollars if their efforts succeed. But it's not impossible to win an uphill battle. And the fact that the playing field isn't level now doesn't mean that it won't ever be level. There is, for example, nothing but culture to stop a country from banning some or all forms of advertising, banning corporate donations to politicians, preventing former politicians from working as lobbyists, or requiring our elected representatives, who are of course employed to make decisions on our behalf, to provide real-time updates on who they are meeting (on our behalf) and what they are discussing (on our behalf).

While such changes may be outside the Overton window in most countries at the moment, one thing that is certain is that the window will shift in the coming decades.

But which way will it shift? As former White House chief of staff Rahm Emanuel once said, 'Never let a good crisis go to waste.'

BIG COMPANIES AREN'T EVEN THAT BIG

As discussed above, far more people work in small businesses than in big businesses. While it serves the interests of those who own lots of shares in big companies for the public to believe that what is good for big business is good for the economy, in fact there is little overlap.

A lot more people in most nations work for themselves than for the biggest companies in their country. In the United States, for example, 53 per cent of people work for organisations with fewer than ten employees.[39]

Some small businesses are well run, have loyal and well-paid staff, and offer both job security and flexibility to their workers. And some are terribly run, underpay their staff and exploit the vulnerability of their workers. Some medium-size and large businesses sit across both these categories. Many people who work for themselves love the freedom and flexibility of it, while many others are self-employed out of necessity.

It's impossible to say what size businesses are the best employers, and the academic literature on what makes for good workplace culture is as diverse as it is voluminous. But a good workplace culture includes strong legal protections, good alternative job prospects, and trust between managers and workers. Put simply, culture is more important than size.

IF ONLY THERE WAS AN ALTERNATIVE TO CORPORATE CAPITALISM

The first customer-owned 'credit unions' started taking deposits and making loans in Germany in the 1850s. In Italy, the People's Bank of Milan opened in 1865, and in 1872 the Co-Operative Wholesale Society formed in England. Credit unions, building societies and mutually owned banks now employ hundreds of thousands of people and hold billions of dollars in deposits.

Yet during the GFC, many people expressed frustration at the lack of alternatives to the multinational banks, which care only for their shareholders, often at the expense of their customers and communities. Member-owned and not-for-profit banks, by contrast, are generally required to reinvest any surplus they generate back into their communities.

While not-for-profit organisations don't (of course) announce large profits each year, that does not mean that they do not make a large contribution to economic activity and community wellbeing. In the United States, for example, the YMCA employs more than 20,000 full-time staff and has 600,000 volunteers. In Australia, the Uniting Church–owned aged-care provider UnitingCare employs

over 35,000 people. This 'charity' and the Anglican
Church's aged-care provider, Anglicare, together employ
more than 60,000 people – more than total employment
in the Australian coal industry.

Charities, not-for-profits, co-ops, member-owned corporations, partnerships and a wide range of other legal and
economic structures employ a large proportion of the workforce in all developed countries. They provide everything
from health and education to transport and tourism. They
produce and sell food, and they provide crisis support. Quite
literally, they are vital in the provision of 'essential services'.
And if you want them to play an even bigger role, there are
several things you can do about it: use more of their services,
lobby your employer or your local government to use them
more, or set up a new organisation to do something new.

I know, I know: we can't all work in aged care or help
the homeless. That's true. But it is also true that we can't
all work in ballpoint pen factories and we can't all work
as corporate lawyers or merchant bankers (whatever that
means). Arguments of this sort ('We can't all sell each
other coffee!'), which are used to trivialise the economic
contribution of both not-for-profits and the service sector more generally, have no economic foundation. Indeed,
there are whole economies where almost 'nothing real' is
produced, such as the economy of Wall Street, or the economy of some Caribbean tax havens. Services, whether they
are provided by tax lawyers or charities, are as real a form

of economic activity as the production of food that gets thrown in the bin.

THE PUBLIC SECTOR HAS ALREADY BEEN INVENTED

No one having a heart attack would think that health services aren't a real part of the economy. Of course it's true that we can't all work in hospitals, but no coalminer or merchant banker having a cardiac arrest is likely to wish we all worked in coalmining or merchant banking. While capitalism is often defined as the pursuit of self-interest, the fact is that, even in a 'free market', we're all in this together; we just can't quite agree on the shape of 'this', or what a fair distribution of 'this' would look like.

Almost all of a society's most important services are provided by the public sector. Some countries have experimented with private police forces, private fire brigades and even private water suppliers, but the overwhelming majority of communities have settled on a preference for 'socialist' provision of essential services. While the principle of 'the user pays' is present in most countries – even when it come to some state services – few societies have opted for a user-pays model when it comes to access to sewerage. Most people really, really want their neighbours to dispose of their waste properly – and that usually means a sewer. Communities that don't publicly fund the disposal of human waste generally face outbreaks of cholera from time to time.

Publicly provided services don't just make our societies function well, they also drive economic activity. Publicly funded research around the world has given us everything from radar and GPS satellites to Wi-Fi and the Google algorithm. The idea that only private-sector activity 'creates' wealth or jobs is as ridiculous as the assertion that the ratio of public-sector spending to GDP is, in any sense, a meaningful indicator of economic efficiency.

Despite the rhetorical aspiration to get government 'down to the size where we can drown it in the bathtub', there is no country in the world that does not have a public sector.[40] In fact, it is only possible to have some form of capitalism after the state, and its public servants, have come into existence. You can't have property rights without judges and police; you can't have judges and police without taxes; and you can't have taxes without an army of public servants to collect them.

The fairytale version of free-market economics found in most textbooks starts with the market forces of supply and demand living peacefully in a Garden of Eden until the snake of the public sector shows up to ruin the 'equilibrium'. But any historical study of how markets came about makes clear that it was the snake that built the garden. Long before there were free markets, there were bandits and thieves who discouraged people from producing and selling large quantities of anything, out of fear that their wares would be stolen long before they were sold. When unelected tyrants began to offer secure property rights in exchange for tax on trade, merchants flocked to the heavily taxed marketplace rather than take their chances in the tax-free but dangerous wilderness.

In both Austria and Sweden, the public sector accounts for more than half of GDP. That is, more than half of all the goods and services in those countries are produced by entities owned by the state. But these nations still have capitalist economies. People are free to own private property and to profit from its use. Indeed, despite what many would describe as its high taxes, Sweden boasts one of the world's best-known transport companies (Volvo) and one of the world's best-known home goods companies (IKEA). It has also given the world Electrolux, Ericsson and Spotify. It's almost as if having a large public sector doesn't prevent the private sector from innovating, exporting, employing people or anything else …

NORTHERN EUROPE DOES EXIST

Any new society or new economy will be built by the one we already have. A new economic system, complete with new rules, new norms and new infrastructure, will never appear out of thin air, complete and ready for use. Just as the Industrial Revolution was built with the tools of an earlier era, the economy of the late twenty-first century will be built with the tools and structures we have today.

It's hard to reform capitalism, or smash it, if you can't be sure exactly what it is and which bits of it are failing and which bits of it are worth keeping. If capitalism is supposed to mean 'a society with no government', well, that dream died long ago. Conservative politicians are very happy for governments to regulate people's sex lives, marriages, recreational drug use and the movement of people across borders. They might want to see less public money spent on health, education and welfare, but they have no apparent desire for governments to stop regulating our behaviour or spending our money on defence. Rather, as we should expect, there is an ongoing democratic debate about what kind of governing our elected representatives should do.

Capitalism is simultaneously everywhere and nowhere. It includes countries such as Madagascar, where the public sector employs only 2 per cent of the workforce, but it also includes Sweden. That both these economies can be described as capitalist points to either the adaptability of the term or its meaninglessness. Either way, for those who wish for an alternative to capitalism, could an achievable goal, in the short term at least, simply be to strive for a public sector as large and vibrant as those of the northern European countries? Indeed, even Swedes looking for alternatives to capitalism could pursue a public sector that accounts for 60 per cent of GDP, or even 70 per cent.

The flexibility of the term capitalism has made it virtually impossible to have a constructive democratic debate about what a country should do more of and what a country should do less of. Proponents of taxing polluters and spending more on education are typically accused of 'abandoning free-market capitalism', wanting to turn their country into 'Communist China' and so on.

While the idea of capitalism is often linked in the public debate to free markets and small governments, the reality is that capitalism, in all its diverse forms, relies on the existence of regulation, and governments to enforce those regulations. As we have seen, many of the enormous banks that many people associate with free-market capitalism only survive today because governments were willing to bail them out. More broadly, without a complex regulatory structure and government guarantees, much of the banking system of capitalist economies would not exist in the first place. Virtually everyone accepts that governments have an important role to play in regulating behaviour, collecting taxes and providing public services. A phoney debate about whether capitalism is good or bad crowds out room for a more useful public debate about which kinds of regulation and services we want more of and which we want less of. The fact that so many Northern European countries collect so much more tax than most developed countries, while still falling into the category of capitalist countries, is clear proof that those who want to significantly reshape the US, UK, Canadian or Australian economies can do so with ease. While debating the theoretical merits of capitalism and socialism might be fun for some, the simple fact is that you can radically change the shape of an economy without having to change the label you attach to it.

REVOLUTIONS NEED CLEAR GOALS, NOT CLEAR LEGISLATIVE AMENDMENTS

Just as the fight about whether GDP growth is good or bad has distracted people from conversations about which aspects of society they would like to see grow and which decline, debates about whether the market or the government is best placed to produce all goods and services have got in the way of a more important enquiry: which goods and services are best provided by the public sector, which goods and services are best provided by the private sector, and what kinds of regulation do we want to impose on private producers?

The world is full of alternatives to corporate capitalism. But just as restaurants don't offer their diners every possible dish, politicians don't present all possible options for economic and social reform to the voters who elect them.

Those who wish to cure the world of affluenza need to feel confident that myriad options exist, that social and economic change is the one thing that is certain, and that a quick look at other countries is all the proof you need to know that there are always alternatives.

But the fact that options exist does not mean they will be easily or effectively applied in new settings. As a country's laws both reflect and reshape a country's culture, it can sometimes be impossible to predict how and when change will occur. For example, in 1964 the US National Bureau of Standards stated that it would embrace the metric system. In 1968 the US Congress authorised a three-year study into the feasibility of metrification, which concluded such a shift would be beneficial. In 1975 the US Congress passed the Metric Conversion Act. And today in the US nearly all road signs express distance and speed limits in miles, not kilometres. Success in changing the law is quite different from success in changing behaviour.

Similarly, Australia has committed to the Paris objectives of reducing global greenhouse-gas emissions, but the Australian government continues to subsidise the construction of new coalmines; Canada has made similar commitments while encouraging the extraction of enormous amounts of oil from its tar sands.

Sometimes it is easier to change the law than it is to change the culture and sometimes it is easier to change the culture than it is to change the law. Those who want to reshape the economy need not divide on the issue of whether it is better to change laws or change behaviour, communicate evidence or communicate messages, or work at the community level or the global level. On the contrary, those who can agree on the direction of change that is necessary should also agree that work in all those domains is necessary and important. While there is no silver policy or political bullet that can change the world, there is a single poison pill that can kill any movement: the idea that there is only one thing that needs to change in order for everything to change.

No one 'invented' the national or global economies we interact with today: they evolved slowly out of the past, as millions of people made millions of choices and decisions. Those who want major change do not have to take responsibility for designing utopia; they only need to pursue the changes that they believe will make things better, steer away from those they think will make things worse, and work with others who share their goals even if they don't share their priorities. The future is full of alternatives we haven't yet rolled out – the only thing up for grabs is who will choose them.

Leanne Minshull

Last year, for the first time in human history, more people lived in cities than outside them. I grew up in the inner-city of Sydney and by the time I started commuting to work, all the transport options that I had to choose from were either expensive, stressful, slow, over-crowded or a combination of all four. It wasn't until I moved to Amsterdam that I discovered I had been forced to choose from a poor set of options. I soon realised that people who had shaped different cities had made radically different choices to the ones made by those who shaped Sydney. I also quickly realised what an impact such choices can have on you personally, and on the character of the city itself.

Growing up in Australia I heard stories of Nordic cities where earnest northern Europeans whizzed about on their pushbikes in the depth of winters, but it wasn't until I moved to Amsterdam that I understood what made them so happy with themselves. Riding my bike around my new home made me richer, healthier and less stressed, but even more than that, I felt like a kid again, master of my own destiny, ready for adventure and beholden to no one. Spontaneous invitations from friends across town became an opportunity for a catch-up rather than an insurmountable logistical challenge. I felt like someone who had found religion or discovered Tupperware and I wanted everyone in Australia to experience what it felt like to live in a city where people, not cars, were king.

Then I started to feel angry about why the choices offered in the country of my birth were so expensive and inconvenient. Cities don't just happen; they are shaped by people, ideas, history, money and power. I began to wonder how it was that Amsterdam had ended up so people-friendly, and which people I should be thanking for it. The answer was as liberating as my bike.

I soon discovered that in the 1950s and '60s Amsterdam, like many industrialised cities, was being transformed by people who made money from making and selling cars. Car ownership increased, roads were hastily constructed and in 1971 more than 400 children were killed in traffic accidents across the Netherlands. People – particularly mothers – organised and agitated. They took direct action by holding dinner parties in the middle of roads, claimed part of the road for bicycles by painting lanes overnight and holding mass demonstrations. Many of the police, cyclists themselves, were sympathetic to the cause. Councils instigated car-free Sundays and constructed curvy roads with multiple bumps, designed to make driving slow.

Fast-forward four decades and the Netherlands is the undisputed cycling centre of the economically developed world. Over one-third of all trips made in Amsterdam are made on a bike and the country has over 30,000 kilometres of bike paths.

Bikes aren't convenient for everyone, but neither, of course, are cars. As more of us live in cities it's more important than ever that we demand that those cities work for all of us. We don't need 'bike-friendly cities', we need bike-friendly city residents who demand that their elected representatives offer their citizens a broad range of choices. If it was made safe and convenient to ride bikes around Sydney, it is hard to believe that fewer people would choose to ride a bike in Sydney's spring than choose to ride a bike in Amsterdam's winter.

Leanne Minushull grew up in car-centric Australia but lived for four years in Amsterdam, working for Greenpeace International. She is the director of the Australia Institute Tasmania.

8

Evaluating New Ideas for Your New Society

'War is the realm of uncertainty; three-quarters of the factors on which action in war is based are wrapped in a fog of greater or lesser uncertainty. A sensitive and discriminating judgement is called for; a skilled intelligence to scent out the truth.'

Carl von Clausewitz

Did you study the right subjects in school? Is it better to have no kids, one, two, three or more? Are you sure you are living in the right house for you right now? Did you choose the right city to live in? Should you have quit your job ten years ago? How do you know you made the right decisions? How can you be sure that you have maximised the rate at which your happiness is growing? What numeric indicator do you or your family use to make big decisions, track progress and plan the future? For me, as for most people, the answer is simple: 'None.'

Indicators, whether of the steps walked in the last day or of GDP growth in the last year, can provide information on how far we have travelled, but no simple indicator can help individuals or countries decide what they should be aiming for. As we've seen, the speed of economic growth is no indication that a country is heading in the right direction.

But despite (or perhaps because of) the lack of simple indicators, most parents can make important decisions with long-lasting implications for their children. And, of course, those same parents are simultaneously making myriad other important decisions, often with poor information to hand, about things that affect their lives, and possibly the lives of others. As we saw in Chapter 6, the idea that national leaders can make big decisions without reference to simple indicators is not new: kings, prime ministers and presidents were making big calls long before GDP was invented.

Those who wish to cure themselves, their community or their country of affluenza might choose to measure their progress in the number of food miles in what they eat, the size of their carbon footprint or the number of years since they last bought petrol. But while such conscious consumerism may help some people to monitor their behaviour and stay motivated, no such indicators are actually required to help individuals reshape their lives or their economy. Just as few parents keep score of their progress as parents, there is no need to keep score of the net impact of your individual decisions. The proof of the pudding, as they say, is in the eating.

The lack of a summary quantitative indicator to help us decide whether we should move house before our kids hit high school – or whether we should take the pay rise and the long hours, or take a lower-paid job closer to home – doesn't mean that all our decisions are random or reckless. The simple fact is that, for something as complex as our personal and family lives, the best we can do is collect the available information, think about our options, ask for advice from those we trust and then make a decision that feels right, based on our principles and culture. Most of us are willing to accept that other people with access to the same information might make different decisions. And most of us are willing to admit that while we hope the decisions we make today will make us and our family happy and healthy in the future, we can't ever be absolutely sure.

THE FOG OF LIFE

It is not just generals who must operate under a fog of uncertainty, and it is not just generals who, having collected as much information as possible, must use their judgement to decide upon the best course of action. Making big decisions amid uncertainty is the downside of the freedom and choice that most people say they want. In our home lives, our work lives and our democratic lives, we can collect a wide range of information and develop indicators of progress, but ultimately we must decide which way to go. And in the absence of perfect information, we can toss coins or we can apply a set of principles to help us make decisions that, we hope, are consistent and mutually reinforcing, and prepare us for the decisions and adversities we are yet to confront.

In a world of rapidly changing technology and culture, though, how do we pursue long-run change? How do we identify long-run priorities, choose good policies to achieve those goals, and engage in democratic and community processes in ways that still leave us time to pursue our passions, enjoy our friends and family and read a good book every now and then? How do we choose what to worry about and what to do about those worries?

Affluence gives us an incredible range of options. Just as we can choose from hundreds of brands of yoghurt, there is an infinite array of policy and cultural problems, and possible solutions, that a dedicated citizen might dedicate their life to pursuing. But there is also the strong possibility that many people, having become overwhelmed, disheartened or simply bored by such a process, will opt out. Which is, of course, what those who like the status quo are hoping will be the case.

This chapter provides a big-picture map to help you navigate the difficult terrain of democratic choice-making. Like any map it must conceal much detail in order to focus attention on the most significant landmarks. No map is perfect.

The following criteria can't tell you what kind of life or community you should pursue, but hopefully they can help you determine better and worse policies and ideas to pursue the world you want to live in. In a democracy none of us is entitled to live in exactly the world we want, but in a democracy there is no reason to expect that if most of us want big change, we can't have it.

THE PERSONAL IS POLITICAL

Conservatives often compare running a country to running a household. But your household doesn't have the capacity to print its own currency, wage war on its neighbours and detain or kill those who don't play by its rules, so the comparison doesn't stand up to much scrutiny. But as a metaphor it is powerful, and conservatives use it for a reason: it works.

Like all metaphors, maps and rules of thumb, the idea that running a country is like running a household is a deliberate simplification, designed to help people understand something big and complex with reference to something small and familiar. The problem isn't the use of this metaphor to help people better understand the macro economy or the government; it's the fact that the metaphor is abused in order to confuse people about those things.

As painful as it might be for many academics and bureaucrats to hear, the truth is that humans prefer simple

metaphors and analogies to complicated economic modelling and cost/benefit analyses. Ironically, many of those
who yearn for a greater reliance on economic or scientific evidence in public debate seem determined to ignore
decades of psychological and linguistic evidence about
how humans accumulate and process information. ('Who
cares if the evidence says just talking about evidence is
ineffective? Now, listen to me talk about the evidence …')

As writers such as George Lakoff have long noted,
it is no accident that conservatives frame debates about
government budgets in terms of household budgets, and
frame debates about law and order in terms of the consequences of 'sparing the rod and spoiling the child'. All the
criminologists in the world, citing all the studies in the
world, have done nothing to persuade conservative voters that longer prison sentences are neither an effective
nor efficient way of reducing crime. But tough-on-crime
politicians keep getting tougher, not because this works
to discourage the criminals but because it works to send a
powerful signal to voters about 'whose side' the politician
is on. The fact that preventing crime and raising children
don't actually have much in common, or that managing a
national economy is not really like managing a household
budget, doesn't mean that it's impossible to have a meaningful conversation with voters about crime or consumer
spending that starts with household examples. Scientists
use simple analogies and metaphors all the time to help

people understand complicated scientific issues. Again, the problem isn't the use of simplifying analogies or metaphors; it's the abuse of them in order to mislead people.

For example, the claim that rising public debt means that a government is 'living beyond its means' is politically powerful, if economically meaningless. Academic economists know that. Treasury officials know that. And most of the politicians making such claims know that. But when progressive critics attack conservatives for using simplistic analogies they are actually falling into a conservative trap. In dismissing conservative metaphors as simplistic, rather than presenting better metaphors, progressive critics of conservative economic management simultaneously steer away from using the most effective tools of mass communication while displaying themselves as 'out of touch' with 'common sense'.

A more effective approach for progressives who want to talk about government budgets or the macro economy would be to start from the premise that households do know how to make good decisions, and to remind people that households regularly go into debt to fund education, cars, houses and everything in between. Like householders, the issue facing governments is not whether debt is good or bad, but whether or not the things being invested in are helping to achieve long-term goals. Just as it makes no sense to buy a house only after you have saved up the full price, so it makes no sense to delay the construction of schools, roads, hospitals, train lines, aircraft carriers or anything else that will deliver long-term benefits just because the government of the day does not have ready cash on hand to pay for it.

When used well, household analogies like this can make a useful contribution to public debate. Let's look at another example. Most households understand that you can't get rich by selling the family farm. Critics of the sale of public assets to help 'balance the budget' would probably achieve more if they relied on folksy household metaphors than if they started an ideological debate about the role of the public sector in a mixed economy.

Looked at from another point of view, the fact that some people use household analogies inappropriately or dishonestly is not evidence that the use of complicated economic modelling or cost/benefit analyses will always lead to helpful or honest public debate. Indeed, it is far more likely that heavy reliance on complicated economic models will lead to a lower quality of public debate, and even fewer people feeling that their opinions count, than if experts and non-experts are required to develop some shared language and metaphors that do help to propel public debate forward.

Whether a country's public debate revolves around the use of kitchen-sink metaphors, cost/benefit analyses or anything else does not change the fact that it is as difficult as it is necessary to find a way to engage millions of people in national conversations about their country's goals and priorities, and the policies that might be adopted to achieve them. And – at the risk of using a potentially misleading household analogy – debates made up of lies and shouting are unlikely to deliver the best possible decisions.

The premise of this chapter is that the principles people use to tackle affluenza in their personal lives should be consistent with the principles that communities and nations use. That is, while a person's choice of personal transport is in no way perfectly analogous to a city's or a country's choice of a transport system, that does not mean that the *principles* by which citizens make their personal and communal choices cannot, or should not, have much in common.

PRINCIPLES FOR TACKLING AFFLUENZA

I. First, do no harm

Back before anaesthetic and antibiotics, the ancient Greeks codified the objective of medical treatment in the Hippocratic oath, the core principle of which was to do no harm. It remains good advice for those trying to cure themselves, or their society, of affluenza or anything else.

Every time someone buys a product, uses a service or casts a vote, they send a signal to themselves, to producers and to other citizens about what they want to see more of and what they want to see less of. Those who want a world in which there is no ivory trade should not buy ivory. Consumer boycotts have a long and successful track record. As hundreds of millions of people have gradually stopped smoking in developed countries, the political power of the tobacco industry has been significantly reduced. Don't support financially what you oppose ethically.

2. Some change is better than no change

The fact that you want the world to cut greenhouse-gas emissions doesn't mean that you shouldn't own a car. But if you want the world to move in a particular direction, you can send a clear signal through your spending and your political choices that you are willing to move in that direction yourself. And you can't keep it a secret. Your voice matters as much as your vote and your wallet.

Producers and politicians can show leadership, but unless citizens and shoppers show their support at the ballot box or cash register, those politicians and companies won't be leading much for long.

While it can be hard for individuals who live a long way from public transport to stop buying petrol, it is not that hard to switch to a smaller, more fuel-efficient car, or to share rides, or to plan trips that kill two birds with one stone, or to work from home one day per week. And you oughtn't be surprised that local politicians do nothing to provide more public transport if you have never spoken to one about how important such an investment would be to attracting or retaining your vote.

Everyone knows how to consume less petrol, electricity or meat, but not everyone appreciates the potential of small changes by large groups to spark national or even global shifts. Electricity use per person and oil consumption per person has been declining in countries such as the United States and Australia for over a decade.[41] Such shifts in energy use not only reduce greenhouse-gas emissions but also the commercial appeal of new investment in coalmines and oil wells, and in turn reduce the relative political power of the fossil-fuel lobby. If just 20 per cent of people used 20 per cent less energy, that translates into a 4 per cent fall in household energy use. Given that most industries always expect growth, even small changes can have big effects.

Defenders of the status quo often say that no one who owns a petrol-powered car can credibly argue that we need to significantly reduce our society's use of fossil fuels. (Interestingly, the same people often simultaneously argue that those who drive electric cars are privileged and wealthy 'virtue signallers'.) By that logic, anyone who thinks taxes are too high must want them to be cut to zero, and anyone who wants more money spent on defence must want all money to be spent on defence. In reality, some change is demonstrably better than none.

Billions of people deciding to use less petrol, eat less meat, buy less bottled water and spend the money they save on services, information and experiences will have an enormous impact on the shape of the economy. Indeed, the shape of the economy is determined primarily by just such choices. And with reshaped economies come reshaped politics. The horse industry was once powerful and the car industry a mere minnow.

3. It's not about sacrifice and denial; it's about saving money and having a better life

Few vegetarians crave meat. Few meat-eaters in Western countries crave dog meat. And few people who understand how celebrities, advertising and culture make things such as handbags or cars seem prestigious crave the latest expensive consumer goods.

Instead of buying bottled water, remind yourself in the morning that you will get thirsty during the day and fill a bottle at home. While it may take some effort to change the habit, if you are finding it a struggle to anticipate that you will get thirsty each day, or if you really enjoy the intrinsic value of buying bottled water, you probably aren't ready to treat your affluenza yet. But remember, some change is better than none. If you stop buying water each day but find yourself reaching for a bottle in a shopping centre one day because you can't find a drinking fountain, that doesn't make you a hypocrite. But hopefully it does make you write a letter to a politician asking for drinking fountains to be placed in all public spaces.

If owning something will make you and your family very happy for a long time, and if you can afford it, you should probably go and buy it. But if it is the act of buying that you hope will temporarily cheer you or your kids up, then you should think again. Curing affluenza doesn't require us to live in an empty house (although many find such minimalism relaxing), nor does it require us to go without necessities or luxuries. On the contrary, curing affluenza requires us to love, cherish, repair and re-purpose our material possessions. Why would anyone throw away something they love? If people buy only the things they need or love, they will buy fewer things, keep them for longer, have more time and money to spare, and consume far less of the world's scarce resources. A society that is tackling affluenza doesn't have to deny itself any pleasure except the dubious thrill of the purchase and its brief afterglow.

Just as there is no harm in eating a piece of chocolate or the occasional slice of cake, there is no harm in buying nice things that give you pleasure for years or decades. Watches, jewellery, furniture and art made centuries ago still make many people happy today. The only thing preventing today's manufacturers from making things that will last for centuries is a culture that values novelty. While consumerism is based on the transient thrill of the new, materialism is based on love of the old.

Rather than feel guilty about materialist pleasures, the way we love our objects – the care with which we select them, maintain them, repair them and hand them on when we are finished with them – should be a source of pride. A society that is shaking off a bad case of affluenza will accord status to those objects that are long-loved rather than recently purchased. We know how to do it for jewellery and vintage cars; only culture is stopping us from applying the same approach to housing, furniture, clothes and appliances.

4. Services are good for you

While laughter might not always be the best medicine, there is overwhelming evidence that it is often good medicine. In turn, there is no doubt that going to see a comedian, going to the movies or downloading an enjoyable television series is good for your health. Doing so also encourages jobs that don't require the consumption of lots of natural resources.

As individuals and societies become wealthier, they tend to spend an increasing proportion of their income on services such as health care, education and aged care. For people who have met their material needs for food, clothing and shelter, it makes sense to invest in lengthening and improving their quality of life. But while not many economists or politicians would criticise wealthy people for increasing their spending on luxury cars or jewellery, the fact that wealthy countries are spending a growing proportion of their national income on health and education is often described as a sign of inefficiency. It is, of course, no such thing. But rising expenditure on health and education is usually met by a growing public sector, the least profitable component of GDP.

The fact that, as incomes rise, people want to spend a larger proportion of their income on services is a good thing. The fact that growth in demand for health and education leads to growth in the size of the public sector is no more evidence of inefficiency than the fact that growth in income leads to increased expenditure on luxury cars. Indeed, in the long run, public investment in health and education will likely deliver more lasting economic benefits than private spending on Rolls-Royces.

Similarly, to the extent that services (whether provided publicly or privately) are typically more labour-intensive and less carbon-intensive, and require far fewer natural resources to produce and create far less material waste, a shift away from goods and towards services will lighten the pressure of human activity on the natural environment.

Put simply, if you have to make a choice between services and stuff, take the services.

5. When you are full, stop consuming

Just as your stomach should tell you when you have eaten enough, your cupboards and your garage should tell you when you have consumed enough. And when you have enough stuff, stop buying it. If your last batch of stuff managed to fill a hole in your cupboard but not in your life, it's pretty likely that the next batch of stuff won't help either.

If you can't afford to buy all the things you and your family really need, the easiest way to reduce your cost of living is to buy less stuff, or to buy stuff with less expensive labels on it. But what if you can afford to buy all the things you and your family really need? The answer is the same: the easiest way to improve your quality of life is to reduce your cost of living by buying less stuff, or stuff with less expensive labels on it.

After breaking the habit of buying more than your cupboards can handle, you might find yourself in the luxurious position of being able to buy more leisure. For example, a 2 per cent wage rise is equivalent to a week's paid holiday. And while you will pay tax on your 2 per cent wage rise, your 'holiday rise' will be tax-free.

If your appetite for stuff is really waning, you might like to push for a nine-day fortnight, which usually comes with a 10 per cent pay cut. Or perhaps you'd prefer a 50 per cent increase in the length of your weekend? A four-day work week usually comes with a 20 per cent pay cut – but, again, that 20 per cent was taxable and your leisure time isn't.

Think of working fewer hours as donating a job to someone else. If millions of people did it, we would all buy a lot less stuff and create a lot more jobs. Win-win for us, but a big loss for the people who make large profits by selling us stuff we don't really need or want.

6. Get yourself and your country into better shape

No single person is in charge of the shape of the economy, but every person with an income has the potential to influence its shape in both the short and the long term. Just as hundreds of millions of people deciding to pay other people to make them coffee has transformed shopping strips over the past two decades, if hundreds of millions of people choose to buy expensive electric cars instead of expensive 'sports cars' or 'sports utilities', they will fundamentally reshape the car industry, the oil industry and the electricity industry.

While working fewer hours or taking longer holidays is a simple solution to the problem of having too much stuff and not enough time, it's not always simple to negotiate such a solution. So if you are in the luxurious position of getting paid a lot more money than you need to meet your material needs, but for some reason you or your boss can't countenance you working less and earning less, what can you do?

Traditionally the simple answer is to donate money to charities, causes or research you support. Such generosity can and does significantly reshape our societies and economies. And if you believe that your donation alone isn't enough to make a tangible difference, why not talk five of your cashed-up friends into joining you? I assure you as the former CEO of a philanthropically funded organisation that the day a group of people ring to ask if you would like to meet to talk about what else the organisation could do if it had another $50,000 is a good day. Supporting the arts, research, advocacy or charitable services delivers a lot of people far more lasting happiness than adding the expensive paint option to a new car or buying the most expensive vitamin pills on the market.

A less talked-about option is to squander your own money strategically in ways designed to help reshape the economy. For those who want to start to cure their affluenza but can't quite see themselves giving a large slab of their spare money away, there is still the opportunity to shift consumption patterns away from disposable stuff and towards either services or long-lived assets that have socially useful consequences. For example, spending a lot of money on an expensive electric car or an enormous photovoltaic solar array for your roof is better for the shape of the economy than spending the same amount on a bathroom or kitchen renovation. Early adopters of socially useful technologies such as electric cars and home battery systems have helped lower their cost and speed up their roll-out.

Finally, if you have so much money that you are worrying about what to waste it on, don't cry poor, don't demand tax cuts and don't allow others to suggest that unless taxes are cut, rich people won't want to work anymore. Voting for higher taxes is not just another way to donate to those that need it, it is a way to ensure that everyone else who can afford to does likewise.

As discussed above, while working less is a good way to redistribute work and income, getting paid a lot of money to do a full-time job you love is not the worst problem to have. If you are 'burdened' with too much money, don't feel bad about it – try to do as much good with it as you can.

7. Flatter is fairer

In a famous thought experiment the philosopher John Rawls challenged people to design a world in which the distribution of income among nations, individuals, races and genders was sufficiently fair that they would choose to be born into such a world without knowing in advance whether they would be born black or white, smart or slow, in a rich country or a poor one.

Kids born to wealthy parents in wealthy countries hit the jackpot, but the vast majority of the world's population, by definition, have no such luck. And while there have been significant improvements in life expectancy and educational opportunities in many developing countries, the fact is that, according to the United Nations, 783 million people do not even have access to clean drinking water at a time when the bottled water industry is expecting rapid growth in rich countries.

Despite the growing inequality between the rich and the rest, both within countries and between them, there is overwhelming biological evidence that intelligence and creativity are evenly distributed across countries and across the globe. But while innate ability might be evenly distributed, clearly other things are not: access to education, high-quality jobs and even clean water. While no one person, or single country, can bring an end to discrimination, structural disadvantage or global inequality, the consumption and voting decisions of each individual, and the trade and diplomatic decisions of each country, can and do make a difference.

Curing affluenza will, inevitably, free up more resources and create more opportunities for those with the least. The quicker the world moves towards a more equal distribution of resources, the sooner we will all benefit from the intelligence and creativity of billions of people who are currently unable to contribute.

We know how to redistribute money within and between countries. We know how to invest in the public services and amenities needed to ensure that all kids get a good start in life. And, with rapidly growing national income and national waste heaps, we clearly have more resources to tackle such problems if we seek to. While it's true that renovating our kitchens creates work for builders, so too does paying more tax and building more schools. We know how to redistribute not just money, but opportunities. The question is whether we collectively want to.

FROM PERSONAL DECISION TO PUBLIC POLICY: TACKLING THE CULTURE OF AFFLUENZA

Countries don't usually make laws about culture, but they are always making laws that reinforce or reshape their culture. Laws about everything from speeding fines and income tax to food regulation and copyright all have the capacity to define, or refine, national culture. Swedish speeding fines are set as a proportion of the driver's income, reinforcing the notion that those with greater means should make a greater contribution. French food regulation is designed to encourage local food production and consumption. Culture, like the economy, is shaped by the net effect of millions of small decisions.

In turn, those who want to cure the culture of affluenza not only need to reconsider their personal choices, they also need to be ever-vigilant about the way that new rules, regulations, policies and budget cuts might either help or hinder them in their goal of reshaping their community or their country. When the mayor of São Paulo, Brazil's largest city, with a population of more than 11 million, announced a ban on all outdoor advertising in his city, business groups predicted job losses and budget deficits. In reality the city continues to grow and an overwhelming majority of citizens support the 'Clean City Law'. No single law will cure a culture of affluenza, but a wide range of laws can help to stamp it out.

Conversely, laws that allow developers to build football stadiums with no drinking fountains facilitate the culture of affluenza. Not only does forcing participants in public events to buy bottled water oblige them to waste their money, such planning decisions reinforce the cultural norms that sustain consumerist culture.

At a more macro level, a society that takes good care of its unemployed will find it much easier to manage the inevitable economic transitions that will arise in the coming decades than will a society that treats its unemployed with contempt and disdain.

Of course, we should not expect all citizens to have the time to evaluate every piece of local, state and federal legislation and develop a considered view. But most democracies do not rely on, or encourage, such a degree of engagement. On the contrary, just as most households make most decisions based on principles and rules of thumb, when evaluating public policy the principles listed above are a guiding framework rather than definitive rules to be followed. As the principles aim to create *better* outcomes, not outcomes that are definitively *right*, it is inevitable that well-intentioned people will disagree with them, just as well-intentioned parents disagree about whether kids should work for their pocket money or not. This is as it should be.

The following four examples start from the premise that people do have the capacity to reshape their community and that an effective way to pursue such goals is to focus on ideas that simultaneously help change not just laws and budgets, but also culture and expectations.

A MORATORIUM ON BUILDING NEW COALMINES

There is no one simple thing the world can do to rapidly reduce greenhouse-gas emissions. But there are many simple things that we can do to ensure emissions continue to rise. One of the easiest ways to cause more climate change is to keep building new coalmines and drilling new oil wells.

For thirty years there have been global, national and local debates about the need to introduce carbon taxes, emissions trading schemes, renewable-energy subsidies and a range of other policies. But over the same period the world's production of coal – the single largest source of greenhouse-gas emissions – has risen from 4.5 billion tonnes in 1986 to 7.5 billion tonnes in 2016.[42]

In 2015 the president of the small, low-lying Pacific Ocean nation of Kiribati wrote to all world leaders asking them to support a moratorium on the construction of new coalmines. He did not call for the immediate closure of the existing mines that, more than any other activity, were producing the heat-trapping gases that threatened to submerge his country; he simply called for a halt to the construction of new ones. Needless to say, most world leaders who apparently support urgent action to tackle climate change ignored this simple request.

Agreeing that the world needs to stop building new coalmines does not preclude the pursuit of subsidies for renewable energy, or imposing carbon taxes for polluting forms of energy, or any other form of climate policy. On the contrary, as efforts to reduce smoking have shown, although the simultaneous pursuit of several policy changes can seem messy, it is often effective.

Just as banning children from smoking is designed to make a clear point that the activity is harmful, a moratorium on new coalmines sends a clear signal about citizen preferences for the future shape of the economy. The unifying idea is that you can't start going forwards until you stop going backwards.

Let's apply the principles above to this specific proposal.

First, do no harm

If countries were serious about avoiding climate change, they would do less of the things that cause it and more of the things that reduce it. Given that coal is the largest single contributor to global greenhouse-gas emissions, a moratorium on the construction of new mines passes the 'do no harm' test.

Some change is better than none

A moratorium on building new coalmines is not enough to reduce emissions below levels considered safe by climate scientists. But then neither were the commitments made by countries at the Paris Climate Change Conference in 2015, and neither is riding your bike instead of driving your car. The moratorium does, however, pass the 'some change is better than none' test.

It's not about sacrifice and denial. Abstaining from building new coalmines will save money, free up resources for other projects and help protect the natural environment. Given that most of the world's economies have no coalmines in them, it is clearly ridiculous to suggest that regions can't grow without new coalmines. Indeed, given that the world demand for coal fell for three years in a row leading up to 2016, a moratorium on new coalmines would be clearly beneficial for the workers in, and owners of, existing coalmines.

Services are good for you

A world that is building fewer new coalmines will need fewer mine construction workers and will use less energy generated from fossil fuels. In turn, a moratorium on new coalmines would change the shape of the economy, making it 'lighter' and, almost inevitably, more service-oriented, as a greater reliance on renewable energy requires a significant substitution of engineering, information and technological development for material fuel consumption.

When you are full, stop consuming

According to climate science, our atmosphere has already consumed too much carbon dioxide, so it is high time we stopped producing so much of it. And, given the enormous amount of coal-fired energy used to produce stuff that is thrown away, a society that is curing its affluenza needs fewer coalmines anyway, even if climate change weren't a pressing problem.

Get yourself and your country into shape

Countries that are still building new coalmines are hardly working flat-out to reshape their societies and economies in ways designed to reduce greenhouse-gas emissions. Indeed, the construction of new coalmines sends a powerful cultural signal that those in power are yet to take seriously the need to make big changes to meet big problems. Building more of what you want more of, and less of what you want less of, is central to the idea of reshaping the economy. A moratorium on building new coalmines would not prevent dangerous climate change, but it would lead to an increase in the cost of coal, give workers in existing coalmines more time to find a new job, reduce the political power of the coal industry and send an important signal about the future shape of economic activity.

Flatter is fairer

A moratorium on the construction of new coalmines would lead to a reduction in the profits of those seeking to build new mines, and an increase in profits and wages for those who own and work in existing coalmines. In the pursuit of a 'just transition' it makes no sense to encourage young people to acquire new skills and move to new towns to work in new coalmines that will not be able to provide long-term employment, especially when those new coalmines will simply displace coal being produced by existing workers in existing mines. A moratorium on new coalmines is not enough to ensure a just transition for existing coal workers, but by preventing new entrants into the coal industry a moratorium will mean there are more resources available to support existing coal workers.

PUBLIC-SECTOR BANKING

The finance sector has become one of the biggest and most profitable industries in the developed world. It is a major employer of some of the best educated citizens, but it is not at all clear how growth in the size or profitability of the finance sector leads to an improvement in the quality of most people's lives. Indeed, given the fees charged by financial institutions for bank accounts, deposits, withdrawals, loans and other transactions, the banks should properly be seen, in many respects, as the private owners of a private taxation system, in which they can 'clip the coupon' on nearly all private transactions.

While banks once performed the physical function of safely storing money and allowing people to securely transfer large amounts of money to others, most of this formerly physical service is now conducted electronically. And despite the potential for new communications technology to lower both the cost of banking and the barriers for new firms to enter the industry, the finance sector remains highly concentrated and highly profitable.

As most employers now only pay their staff electronically, and many firms only accept payments by credit card or electronic funds transfer, banking has effectively become an essential service that people cannot opt out of, even if they think the costs are too high or the service unsatisfactory. Historically, it was the public sector that provided essential services, in order to ensure their equitable and reliable supply. Although many governments have deliberately privatised their investments in banking, technological change has created new opportunities for the public sector to enter, re-enter or expand its engagement in the finance sector in novel ways.

Consider the following. A bank account and an account with your national tax office are virtually identical from a legal and technological point of view. Both revolve around the linking of a unique identifying number to a name and account balance, along with an ability to charge (or pay) interest. In most countries it is possible for employers to make additional voluntary tax payments on behalf of their employees each pay period (deposits), which citizens can then access once a year via a 'tax return' (withdrawal). In short, in developed countries the computerised system that sits behind the tax system is the equivalent of a simple savings bank account, albeit one with a clunky web interface.

In fact, the degree of 'administrative banking' that governments can provide is far more widespread than the capacity to take deposits, hold funds and facilitate withdrawals. In the United States, Canada, Australia, the United Kingdom, New Zealand and other countries it is possible to get 'loans' directly from the government, either through the tax system or the welfare system, with repayments made automatically through those same systems. Intriguingly, these loans are rarely called loans, with governments often preferring to refer to them as 'advances', 'deferred taxes' or 'temporary supplements'. For example, in Australia, the federal government is willing to lend tens of thousands of dollars to university students (known as the Higher Education Loans Program), to lend up to $1000 to welfare recipients (known as a 'welfare advance') and to offer reverse mortgages to wealthy retirees (known as the Pension Loans Scheme).

When governments already have the computer systems in place, have zero-cost access to the best debt-collection system available (compulsory tax payments) and can borrow at lower rates than private banks, there is no reason, other than ideology, for the public sector not to set up simple 'savings and loan' accounts for any and all citizens who would like them. Citizens opting into the use of existing public infrastructure to provide low-cost banking services would effectively allow them to 'nationalise' the banking system one transaction at a time.

The gradual growth of such an institution would have the potential to significantly reshape the finance sector, the distribution of fees and dividends, and the economy more broadly. Needless to say such an idea would be fought tooth and nail by the owners of existing banks, most likely on the basis that public provision of services is 'less efficient' than private provision.

Developing widespread public competition for private banks would cause no environmental harm, would help shift the shape of the economy towards the public sector and would lead to no increase in material consumption. It could lead to a significant cut in the cost of banking (and living) for customers, and to a significant cut in the proportion of national income going to the owners of bank shares. By demonstrating that well-run public services can be superior to private-sector alternatives, the voluntary introduction of public banking would not only reduce the size (and political power) of the finance sector, it would also embolden those pushing for other, perhaps more ambitious, roles for the state.

WHAT IF GOVERNMENTS HANDED OUT STATUS CREDITS?

Frequent flyers are treated better in some public places than their less well-travelled peers. They get to use express lanes at security, they can board the plane first, and they might even get to wait in a nice lounge with free food and drinks. In an affluent society in which you can nearly always buy yourself out of trouble (if you can afford to), queuing and waiting are very low-status activities. The airlines know that allowing their best customers to jump the queue and breeze past the parents with screaming kids is a cheap way to buy loyalty – and, more importantly, repeat business.

But if airlines can hand out status credits to drive repeat business, in the same way nightclubs put the names of special people 'on the door', why shouldn't governments encourage and reward the 'right' kind of behaviour in similar ways?

The tradition of handing good citizens the 'keys to the city' dates back to the times of walled cities, the gates to which were locked and guarded at night. Those given the keys were not just the recipients of public status, but had the freedom to enter and exit the city at any time, day or night. Their status in the community was accompanied by tangible benefits.

There is nothing to stop a city, a state or a nation from rewarding community volunteers, good Samaritans and people exhibiting bravery or generosity by providing them with both public status and private convenience. Imagine if:

- The best parking spots were reserved for those with 'community status'.

- The best seats at community sporting grounds and theatres were reserved for those with 'community status'.

- In peak-hour traffic, whole lanes were reserved for the use of teachers, nurses, aged-care workers or workers in any other profession that the government said they wished they could reward with a pay rise but couldn't afford to.

While there's no doubt citizens would disagree about which activities deserves status and what rewards would be appropriate, in reality such democratic decision-making is no different to decisions about who is eligible for concession cards, how many car spaces should be reserved for the disabled and who is eligible for public awards for community service.

In a society suffering from a bad case of affluenza, the private sector is the dominant provider of status, and the major recipients of that status are the wealthiest citizens, along with those celebrities who help the rich get even richer by advertising luxury clothes, cosmetics or cars. We could reduce the influence and pervasiveness of advertising by restricting it or requiring more transparency, but a more effective approach would be to make celebrities wait in line behind those citizens we have collectively, and democratically, decided are worthy of status and special treatment.

A community that was willing to award status and other non-monetary rewards to citizens whose ideas and efforts helped to improve social wellbeing could significantly reshape their community without raising taxes, borrowing money or seeking grants. The mere act of beginning a communal conversation about what behaviours might be rewarded, and the best way to reward those behaviours, could in itself strengthen community bonds and encourage higher expectations of local governments.

The strategic use of status by governments could only be harmful if the community sought to reward harmful activities. While awarding status and other non-monetary benefits will do nothing to prevent companies or individuals from doing harm, it has the potential to shift culture away from the individualism of affluenza and towards norms and attitudes that take giving to the community seriously.

REPAIR CULTURE

Imagine if manufacturers and retailers were responsible for providing a full cash refund for products that had broken and, through design or lack of availability of spare parts, could not be repaired.

Imagine if local communities provided shared facilities not just to fix things, but to bring people together in ways designed to help them help each other to fix things. Imagine if the technology of dating apps was used to introduce people with a problem to people with the skills to solve that problem. And imagine if the owners of sheds and spare rooms full of unused stuff could be linked up with people looking for a spare part or a near-new replacement for a much-used appliance or tool.

Providing a physically and technologically safe place for people with broken things and people who like to fix things to come together has little potential to do harm and lots of potential for people to save money and make new friends. While it would take time to change the laws around refunds and repairability, the barrier to encouraging such community action is low and it is highly likely that the lessons of early adopters would help other communities jump-start such activities.

It is likely that different people with different skills, at different stages of their life, would seek to contribute to, and extract from, community repair centres in different ways. Some people may wish to sell their skills, some may want to barter time for things, and some would simply want to donate their time and experience in order to contribute to their community.

While the emergence of 3D printing will make the production of spare parts simpler and cheaper, most of the repair economy would consist of the provision of services. To the extent that repaired items are a substitute for new items, repair culture would likely lead to an overall reduction in material use and an increase in the size of the service sector. To the extent that repaired goods are likely to be cheaper than new goods, repair culture would lead to falls in the cost of living and, for some, provide a source of either income or stuff in exchange for skilled labour.

In the long run, the potential size of the repair economy will be significantly influenced by cultural expectations and the consumer laws that accompany them. While some firms maximise their profits by producing goods that are destroyed when people seek to open them up, if people refuse to buy products that cannot be repaired, firms will eventually change strategy. Changes to consumer laws would obviously speed such a cultural shift, but, as discussed above, the processes of individual change and policy change are often deeply enmeshed and self-reinforcing.

WHAT ELSE SHOULD WE DO?

There is no silver bullet for affluenza. Like influenza, or any contagious disease, affluenza will continue to evolve, its transmission mechanisms will continue to change, and cultural habits as diverse as recreational shopping and humble-bragging about new purchases on social media will continue to shape the rate and severity of its spread.

On the other hand, curing affluenza does not require enormous personal or economic sacrifice; on the contrary, wasting far less time, resources and energy producing stuff that is rarely or never used will make our lives richer, and our economies more efficient and stronger – even if some parts of the economy will shrink or vanish in the way our typewriter and steam engine factories have.

But while curing affluenza will not require much, if any, genuine personal sacrifice, it will require a much larger section of the community to engage not just in social media debates about the personalities and peccadilloes of our political class, but also in debates about the goals and overall direction we want for our country. While policy detail matters to some, policy objectives should matter to everyone. At a personal level we will need to spend more time thinking about what we really need and what we really want. We have built the wealthiest societies in the world and there is nothing to prevent the vast majority of the population from having all of their needs, and most of their wants, met – unless their wants are to perpetually dispose of the things they once said they really wanted.

Alternatives to a society and economy based on consumerism exist in abundance, and new ones are being developed all the time. The first task is to decide that we want change. The second is to see ways of achieving it. The next chapter discusses the third and final step: dealing with those who are determined to block us.

Bill McKibben

Back in 1994 the world's governments pledged to take actions necessary to 'prevent dangerous anthropogenic interference with the climate system' as part of the UN Framework Convention on Climate Change. But in the years that have followed, global emissions have soared – the direct result of government decisions supporting the expansion of the fossil-fuel industries. Already these decisions are breaking some of our planet's largest features. The icecaps are melting and coral reefs are dying off from repeated bleaching. We are seeing harsher droughts, heatwaves and wildfires, and food insecurity is stirring conflict. Lags in the climate system mean even just the emissions we have released so far have locked in worse impacts in decades to come. And yet, after all these years and after all that damage, governments are allowing and facilitating

the expansion of the coal, oil and gas industries that are causing this havoc.

While it is too late to stop climate change altogether, it is not
too late to slow it down. But to take on the power of the biggest
industry ever, we will need to build the biggest ever social movement. We don't just need people to turn off their lights, but to
turn out in the streets. We will need some more brave people to
step up and take action to stop new polluting fossil fuels – to get
out in front of bulldozers, or fracking drills, or the White House,
where in 2011 along with 1200 others, I was arrested protesting
the Keystone XL oil pipeline.

But as that fight made clear to me, any campaign is fight-
ing uphill so long as the industry is viewed as a respectable and
even inescapable part of people's lives. That social licence is
essential to the industry's power over our politics. It needs to
be revoked. That's where the fossil-fuel divestment campaign
comes in.

Divestment is based on a simple idea: if it is wrong to
wreck the planet, then it is wrong to profit from that wreck-
age. People who are serious about stopping climate change
can put their money where their mouths are by avoiding investments in the coal, oil and gas companies whose business
plans are inconsistent with stopping climate change. By shifting their money, people can help to shift the culture as well as
the energy industry.

The climate mathematics are stark. Any reasonable chance
of stopping the worst impacts means leaving the vast majority

of the world's fossil-fuel reserves underground – these reserves that are currently above-ground as assets on the books of the governments and companies that expect to profit from them. Simply put, those plans are inconsistent with a climate that works something like the one in which complex human civilisation developed.

The divestment movement turns this scientific knowledge into something people can do. As individuals we can shift our own money out of services such as banks that invest in fossil fuels to those that don't. Similarly, we can call on our religious, charitable and educational institutions to take a public leadership position consistent with their values. It's not just our money that matters, it's our voice and our leadership.

The growth of the divestment movement has been remarkable. From a few campus divestment campaigns in the US and Australia five years ago, 350.org and other organisations have helped spread this simple idea into a worldwide phenomenon with its own momentum. Local campaigns have won commitments from institutions as varied as Stanford University, the British Medical Association, the Australian Academy of Science, the World Council of Churches and Norway's sovereign wealth fund, which is the world's largest fund.

I've lost count of the number of times I've heard critics dismiss divestment as empty symbolism. Symbols are powerful, and the resistance to divestment only makes that clearer. Divestment has a historical track record, in movements against tobacco and South African apartheid. The stigma from divestment can create conditions for real change, increasing risks of government action and disrupting business conditions. Fossil-fuel companies now cite divestment as a material risk and they are struggling with recruitment as many of the best and brightest students now avoid working for such pariahs.

Keeping fossil fuels in the ground is going to take actions of many forms, on many frontlines. As leaders refuse to do their job, divestment allows people to show leadership from the bottom up, building pressure on governments and business alike and changing the terms of the fight. History is full of mass movements shifting culture, resources and outcomes. The fossil-fuel divestment campaign has given millions of people a powerful way to make themselves heard, and in a functional democracy, nothing is more powerful than that.

Bill McKibben is an author and environmentalist.
His many books include *The End of Nature* and *Oil and Honey*,
and he is a founder of 350.org.

9

So What's Stopping You?

*'Practical men who believe themselves to be quite exempt
from any intellectual influence, are usually the slaves
of some defunct economist. Madmen in authority, who
hear voices in the air, are distilling their frenzy from some
academic scribbler of a few years back.'*

John Maynard Keynes

S wimming against the tide is tiring. Changing
the flow of the tide is exhausting. But both are
possible, and the world we live in today was, in
the most literal sense, shaped by those willing to
buck trends, fight City Hall and drive change.

But to change policy in any significant way, you usually
have to change the culture first. And as anyone who has ever
declared that flared jeans are coming back knows, there is
a big difference between declaring culture will change and
seeing it actually happen. It takes effort, strategy, determination, allies and usually a bit of luck to change a society.
And it takes time.

Just as fish can't taste the water they swim in, it's hard
for individuals to detect the influence of the culture that

surrounds them. It is hard to see how culture shapes our personal choice of which particular necktie to buy. But it's harder still to detect the role that culture plays in so many people's desire to wear a superfluous but symbolically important piece of material around their necks in the first place.

It is, of course, possible that hundreds of millions of men have some innate desire to tie nooses around their necks before they head to their offices. But it's more likely that culture shapes individual choice as much as individual choice affects culture. And what's with the buttons on the sleeve of a suit jacket? When was the last time you saw someone roll up their jacket sleeve? No doubt the makers of buttons are glad you either haven't noticed their unnecessary adornments or you've been too keen to fit in to voice any objection.

Residents of rich countries spend tens of billions of dollars on buttons, perfume, aftershave, lipstick, teeth whiteners, hair gel, hair dye and myriad other aesthetic modifications whose value, status and necessity are entirely culturally determined. But who determined them? Buttons on jacket sleeves are allegedly there to stop men wiping their noses on them. But some men simultaneously display handkerchiefs in their jacket pocket which they are also unlikely to blow their nose on. Who decided on the significance of these accoutrements and for how many more hundreds of years will their decisions shape our consumption patterns?

Symbols matter. Culture matters. Yet many people determined to build support for a piece of 'evidence-based policy' tend to ignore both the cultural tide they are swimming in and the symbolic significance of the change they desire. Those who wish to reshape the world are going to need a lot more than new technologies and new regulations. They are going to need a new culture in which they are confident enough to demand more of the things they want more of and less of the things they want less of – and to stand up against those who are fiercely determined to keep some things the way they are.

THE MARKET DIDN'T DO IT

As we've seen, the idea that the market or global corporations are responsible for big decisions about our economy and society is appealing but misleading. It's always people. A market is simply a place where buyers and sellers come together; it is the people in a marketplace who make decisions. It was a person at Apple who decided to make hundreds of millions of existing phone chargers obsolete. It was a person at Coca-Cola who decided to change the recipe, and a different person who decided to change it back again. It's not the market or a corporation that decides whether to sack thousands of workers, whether to drill for oil in the Arctic, or whether to dump pollution in a river. All those choices are made by people.

Imagine you are at a fish market. It's usually a large, cold, smelly building filled with people who want to buy fish and people who want to sell fish. Now imagine someone asks you, 'What does the fish market want?' While it makes sense to ask what fish buyers and fish sellers want, it is meaningless to ask what the fish market itself wants. All the fish market does is house the people doing the buying and the selling.

Blaming the markets or big corporations for the 'need' to cut taxes – or the 'need' to cut wages, reduce public spending on health, or ignore the threat of climate change – is a deliberate strategy to diminish the role of citizens' voices in shaping their society. It's a bit like claiming that Zeus, Apollo or God will be angry if a society ignores the advice of its high priests. Or that next year's crops will thrive if the farmers give enough of this year's crop to the priests as a sacrifice.

We have built a culture that gives a higher priority to the opinions and desires of some citizens than others. Citizens who can speak confidently about 'how the markets will react' are given a much greater say in public debate than those who can speak confidently about what millions of people think is fair or good or important. By talking endlessly about what the market wants or what the global economy needs, we have created a culture in which the voices and desires of rich people who own a lot of shares take precedence over the desires of working- and middle-class people who rely heavily on public services.

This culture of talking about 'the market' not only amplifies the voices of the small number of people who own a large share of the national wealth, it also leads millions of citizens to censor themselves and refrain from contributing to democratic debate. Just as middle-class Romans didn't enjoy the prospect of angering the gods unnecessarily, many middle-class citizens in rich countries seem to fear angering the markets if they demand that wealthy citizens pay more tax so that all citizens can get better services.

Throughout recorded history, stories have been used to persuade large populations that it's better to stay within the known world and not venture towards the edge of the map, lest they encounter monsters. For too long, the markets and the ratings agencies have been enlisted by the powerful to ensure that public debate about taxes, services and regulation stays within the current Overton window: a culture in which small government is good, lower taxes are better, and public spending is somehow a sign of economic inefficiency.

Deferring to the markets is as irrational as it is undemocratic. And doing so creates fertile conditions for an epidemic of affluenza.

DEMOCRACY CAN DO IT (IT'S DONE IT BEFORE)

To cure affluenza, we will need to rely as much on broad democratic reform as on specific reforms to environmental, workplace or consumer laws. Banning bottled water is, for some, a big ask – but banning corporate donations to political parties would make banning bottled water a lot easier. It would also make reducing fossil fuel use, and many other issues, a lot easier.

It is a lot simpler to invigorate a democracy than it is to drag one into existence, in the face of opposition from kings, generals and tyrants. It is possible to revive a flagging democracy and let citizens know they can influence big decisions about the shape of their society, despite the contempt and hostility of those who profit from the status quo. Those who want to reshape the world will always face resistance. Sometimes it will be fierce, and sometimes brutal. But history says it can be overcome.

Oil is the most profitable commodity in the world and, perhaps unsurprisingly, oil executives have a long history of shaping the culture they operate in to keep the profits flowing. Donating to politicians and funding climate-change sceptics have for decades been 'core business' for those in the oil industry. Indeed, in some countries oil company executives have gone much further, funding militias, bribing politicians and even killing community leaders who stood between the companies and ever-larger profits.

It's not companies that pay bribes or pull triggers – it is individuals. Yet although companies might not be able to think or feel, they are increasingly given the rights of individuals before the law. For example, even though a company has no feelings, it can now be defamed in a growing number of jurisdictions. But one right that companies do not have is the right to vote. And in a democracy the right to vote is a very powerful thing.

As we saw in Chapter 7, at the beginning of the twentieth century legislators in the United States decided to take on J.D. Rockefeller and the other 'robber barons' of the era. They won. In the mid-twentieth century the UK government, as it recovered from six years of total war with Germany, introduced the world-class National Health Service, which was entirely publicly funded. There is no doubt that, were such actions proposed today, the markets would be reported to be furious. But luckily for billions of people, this kind of nonsense wasn't common back then.

When a large proportion of a democracy's population are determined to see change, and willing to switch their vote to parties or politicians committed to delivering such change, almost anything is possible. Democracy is not perfect, but it has shown itself to be capable of driving large changes over a long period of time. That said, democracy itself is a culture. When people lose faith in democracy, they empower the big companies and billionaires they fear have already accumulated too much political power. When a culture has low expectations of its democratically elected representatives and its democratic institutions, it becomes far easier for the minority to prevail over the majority. The last thing a politician who takes major donations from

corporations or who lunches regularly with corporate lobbyists wants is an electorate made up of people who expect
to be listened to, and who have a track record of shifting
their vote when they are ignored.

Speaking of politicians: while few people praise them as
a group, the simple fact is that you can't have a democracy
without them. Similarly, while we might sometimes laugh
at the inefficiency of government, our elected representatives can't turn ideas into actions without a bureaucracy.

But despite the obvious truth that you can't have a
democracy without politicians or bureaucrats, for decades
people have been told that 'all politicians are the same' and
'all bureaucrats are inefficient'. Such criticism might roll
effortlessly off a tired and cynical tongue, but it helps create a culture that has little faith that citizens can reshape
their society.

Only a culture in which we have high expectations – of
both our democratic representatives and our democratic
institutions – can help turn the hopes of citizens into a
reshaped society.

NEOLIBERALISM IS BAD FOR DEMOCRACY

For decades, billions of people have been told by the high
priests of economics and finance that greed and selfishness are
the dominant human motivators, that rational people think
only about themselves, that collective solutions to collective

problems are inefficient, and that rising inequality gives people an incentive to work harder. What could go wrong?

Over the same period, faith in democratic institutions around the world has been falling, and cynicism towards politicians has been rising. While there is no one cause of this decline across different countries with different constitutions, it is hard to believe that endless repetition of the argument that governments are inefficient, that politicians are incompetent, and that faith in the goodwill of others is naive has had no effect on our expectations of elected officials.

A culture that glorifies the pursuit of individual goals is a culture that enables the rapid spread of affluenza. If citizens believe their community will do nothing to help those at the bottom, they have a stronger incentive to claw their way to the top – and even to stand on a few other people to get there. To build a strong sense of community, people need to settle down, engage regularly with their neighbours and develop a sense of shared goals. But many of the preferred policy tools from the neoliberal toolbox do not help bring people and communities closer together; rather, they work to drive people apart. For example, the combination of insecure work that is hard to get and harder to keep and punitive approaches to welfare does more to keep people on their toes than to help them put down deep roots in their communities and workplaces.

A culture that links personal security to personal financial prosperity also encourages the acceptance of affluenza. If you believe that the only way to protect yourself, or your community, is to amass financial assets, then it makes sense to favour what is supposedly good for the economy over what you believe is good for your own family, your health, your environment or your community. And a culture that has been trained to see tax as a burden – both on individuals and on the economy – is a culture that (understandably) will struggle with the idea that collecting more money in tax and spending it on high-quality health, education and transport will lighten the load of modern life. Neoliberalism tells us to trust the market but not our elected representatives.

Markets have played a significant role in human societies throughout recorded history. But the idea that the market should shape our personal and cultural values is a very new one, and very inconsistently applied. Try asking a conservative politician if abortion is legitimate as long as the person seeking the abortion and the person offering the abortion can agree on a fair price. Even in notionally communist countries, markets play a role in what, how and for whom things are produced. The question is not whether markets are good or bad at providing services, but whether they are better or worse than publicly funded services, co-operatively funded services or self-funded services.

Neoliberalism has played a powerful role in shrinking the size of the Overton window in most countries. But a society that wants to abandon neoliberalism doesn't need to invent a new paradigm – it simply needs to restore its faith in the wide range of options, from public provision of services to co-operatives, that neoliberalism has so successfully erased from the policy menu. Similarly, a society that wants to develop an alternative to neoliberalism needs to restore its faith in itself and its institutions, and to develop new ideas, test them, refine them and roll them out over time. It's been done plenty of times before.

YOU CAN'T RESHAPE A TREE WITHOUT SOMETHING SHARP

'*When the carpenter picks up his saw, if wood could talk, it would scream.*'

Robert Schenkkan

If the branches of a tree grew as unevenly as the branches of an economy, the tree would quickly fall over. But those who focus only on the size of economies have become blind to their shape, and therefore to the catastrophic risks such an imbalance can cause.

In rich Western countries, the parts of our economies that generate waste, inefficiency and inequality are bulging while the parts that provide health, education, innovation and a sense of community are withering after decades of deliberate cuts and studied indifference – supposedly all in the name of increasing the efficiency of the economy. Over the same period, the proportion of national wealth held by the nation's wealthiest has grown as rapidly as the piles of wasted consumer goods that, we are told, are essential for a strong economy. The reshaping of economies and the redistribution of benefits when the neoliberal pruners wield the secateurs is no accident, and it certainly isn't random.

Gardeners understand that there are many good reasons to prune a tree. Well-aimed cuts can generate new growth. Old branches can overshadow other, more useful plants. Branches can become diseased. Sometimes dead wood simply needs to be removed. While pruning and reshaping reduces the size of a tree in the short term, when done well it ensures that the tree is fit for purpose. Pruning can speed future growth, increase the amount of fruit produced, ensure that the rest of the garden can grow rapidly, or make the tree into a shape that its owners like the look of. It is up to each gardener to decide on both the form and function of the tree.

The same is true of our society. We must collectively decide on our communal goals and the best way to achieve them. We might not always agree whether the purpose of the tree is to produce fruit or to look neat and tidy. And we might not agree about whether cutting a branch will harm or help the tree. But what we should be able to agree on is that it is not up to the saw to decide which branches need cutting.

As Amory Lovins once said, 'The markets make a good servant but a bad master. And an even worse religion.'

Market forces drove the take-up of the smartphone, which has both been a boon to lost travellers and caused the death of countless distracted drivers. But the fact that the market is an effective tool does not make it an effective designer.

Over the past thirty years, conservative politicians and conservative institutions such as the IMF and World Bank have taken the metaphorical chainsaw of the market to reshape our economies and societies in their preferred image. Based on the belief that the more of our public sector they cut from our society, the faster the rest of the economy would grow, these institutions barracked loudly as politicians around the world cut ruthlessly into the services that lay at the heart not just of many citizens' lives, but of many communities as well.

Some of those who wielded the chainsaw might have genuinely believed that the benefits of 'new growth' would trickle down to those who once clung to the branches they had lopped from the tree. But in reality, as the destruction of whole towns and regions across the world has shown, the reshaped tree is now so unbalanced that it is likely to topple over.

Believing that cutting taxes on high-income earners, cutting public spending on public services and privatising public assets would lead to rapid economic growth that would deliver benefits for all, the proponents of the neoliberal agenda were as confident as they were ineffective. The financial deregulation they championed helped cause the global financial crisis, and their belief that further spending cuts would speed economic recovery only prolonged the pain of hundreds of millions of people who played no role in the banks' recklessness.

The neoliberal architects of the modern economy are proud of their achievements. They worked hard to cut public spending on essential services, cut income support to vulnerable people and, of course, to cut taxes paid by high-income earners.

They have a vision of the shape of society that they prefer, and they have worked tirelessly, as is their right, to shape it in their preferred image. These people, and the institutions they work for, do not need to be persuaded of the case for a change in direction. They need to be ignored by those who are determined to pursue a different vision.

RESHAPING SOCIETY ISN'T PAINLESS, BUT IT DOESN'T HAVE TO BE CRUEL

You can't end whaling without causing job losses for whalers, and you can't burn a lot less coal without employing many fewer coalminers. There is no avoiding the fact that any successful effort to reshape the economy will cause pain for some people. But the amount of pain experienced by those who lose their jobs, their identity or their sense of community when a society is reshaping itself is determined by our social decisions, not by economics. Whether those who lose their jobs are eligible for generous unemployment benefits or custom-made retraining – and whether or not they are treated with respect and dignity by their community – is not decided by the market but by our culture.

As we saw in Chapter 4, the invention of the tractor, the shift from steam to diesel to electricity and the rapid roll-out of smartphones have all led not just to massive job destruction, but to massive cultural and community upheaval as well. Given that there is no scenario in which large numbers of people will not be forced to change their jobs in the coming century, it seems remarkable that anyone could argue that a reason to cause climate change is that it will prevent some people from having to change their jobs.

While it might seem logical and politically tempting to delay, for example, the shift away from coal until a plan is developed to re-employ or relocate each affected coal worker, history suggests that reliance on such planning will be far more effective in delaying the necessary change than in helping the affected workers. Just as no one could have foreseen the impact of smartphones on job creation and destruction, no one can foresee the precise ways in which big shifts in energy production will affect jobs, towns and communities.

A more honest and consistent approach to a just transition for those who work in the fossil-fuel sector is to simply stop building new coalmines, oil rigs and coal-fired power stations that we know will not be needed in the future. By preventing the construction of new forms of pollution, the adjustment for those who already work in those sectors can be made smoother and more predictable. Once we've abandoned plans to keep going backwards, we can then turn our minds to how to plan the transition as we move forwards. And the best way to protect workers displaced by climate-change policy, changes in technology, natural disaster or even just changes in consumer preferences is to treat all citizens well in their times of need. Put simply, climate change or not, there is no economic reason why all workers and communities shouldn't have access to the financial, retraining and other support that we would all hope our kids would receive if they ever lost a job through no fault of their own.

CONCLUSION

> 'You may resist an invading army, but nothing can stop an idea whose time has come.'
>
> **Victor Hugo**

There is nothing economically efficient about borrowing money you don't have, to buy things you don't need, to briefly entertain or impress yourself or others, before you then throw that stuff away. And there is no evidence that speeding up the rate at which we produce and dispose of things is making us happier, healthier or (for most) better off financially.

The end of slavery was a cultural change that brought enormous economic consequences.

Women's pursuit of equality in the workplace also had enormous economic consequences.

Similarly, if in the near future billions of people decide to buy less stuff, consume more services, take longer holidays, pay more tax and demand better public services and infrastructure, they will radically alter their communities, their countries and their world.

No doubt some people will declare that individuals preferring time and services to more useless stuff is 'bad for the economy', but what they really mean is 'bad for the people who profit from selling useless stuff'. No doubt some people might argue that unless we all continue to buy things we don't need, and dispose of them quickly, mass unemployment will ensue.

But the idea that people should keep racking up debt and consuming things made from the world's scarce resources in order to create jobs for their fellow citizens is merely a bizarre inversion of socialist urgings to sacrifice to make the economy strong. If modern capitalism has reached the point where we are being urged to consume more than we need simply in order to keep the show on the road, then it's obviously time to stop and think.

Yes, it's true that a world that buys and discards fewer things will employ fewer people to make them; but wasting less of our time and resources will not make us worse off. On the contrary, the parts of the economy that we don't really need will inevitably shrink, and the parts of the economy that we want more of will grow. If, collectively, we choose to buy more leisure time and less goods and services, there is no reason to believe we would be collectively poorer – even if GDP were to fall.

There is no silver bullet that will cure affluenza. Cultural change takes vision, resolve, patience and confidence. But there is a poison pill that might stop us from curing ourselves: doubt. Many people seem to have absorbed the idea that while the status quo might seem both undesirable and unsustainable, there is no alternative to such a system. As long as people doubt that change is really possible, they will leave the shape of the future in the hands of those who have so ruthlessly cut away those parts of the economy which many people say they want more of. As Bertrand Russell said, 'The trouble with the world is that the stupid are cocksure and the intelligent are full of doubt.'

Every choice you make reshapes your society and your economy. But the choices made by our democratic leaders can drive big changes, and fast. Some people are going to put their hand up to determine the shape of tomorrow's society. Why can't you be one of them?

Acknowledgements

I think life is a team sport. And while writing is a solitary activity, there's a whole team of people supporting and sustaining me.

First, I'd like to dedicate this book to my parents, Jan and Dick, who more than anyone else have supported, encouraged and inspired me throughout my life. I don't know any people who have found such joy with so little stuff, and I don't know any people who are less susceptible to catching even a mild dose of affluenza.

I also owe a huge debt to the staff and financial supporters of my employer, the Australia Institute, which provides me with the most supportive environment for thinking and writing that I could possibly imagine. A special thanks to Ben Oquist for his endless energy and enthusiasm not just for this project, but for the task of pushing new ideas into old debates.

This book would have never been completed without the patient and thoughtful advice and encouragement of

Chris Feik at Black Inc. No one has done more to help me understand what it takes to turn interesting ideas into an interesting book. I hope this volume lives up to his counsel. The book has also benefited enormously from the generous contributions of Bob Brown, Marilyn Waring, Bill McKibben, Craig Bennett, Leanne Minshull, Kumi Naidoo, John Quiggin and Jim Stanford.

And then there are the ever-friendly staff of Canberra's Tilley's Cafe, in which all of this book was written, and the morning regulars who give me the perfect amount of support and solitude.

And finally, thanks to my family for their unfailing support and willingness to accept that I'm more fun to be around after I have spent the day writing.

Endnotes

1   Laura Clark, 'A career? Just make us stars, say children in new survey', *Daily Mail*, 2 October 2009, www.dailymail.co.uk/news/article-1217484/A-career-Just-make-stars-say-children-new-survey.html.

2   International Bottled Water Corporation, 'Bottled water the nation's healthiest beverage', www.bottledwater.org/bottled-water-%E2%80%93-nation%E2%80%99s-healthiest-beverage-%E2%80%93-sees-accelerated-growth-and-consumption.

3   John G Rodwan, Jr, 'Bottled Water 2014: Reinvigoration', *Bottled Water Reporter,* Jul–Aug 2015 issue, www.bottledwater.org/public/BWR%20 JulyAug%202015%20Issue_BMC_2014%20Bottled%20Water%20 Statistics%20Article.pdf.

4   Michael Sivak and Brandon Schoettle, 'Recent decreases in the proportion of persons with a driver's license across all age groups', The University of Michigan Transportation Research Institute report no. UMTRI-2016-4, http://umich.edu/~umtriswt/PDF/UMTRI-2016-4.pdf.

5   Mike Clay, 'How Millennials are driving the shift away from cars', *ABC News*, 20 November 2014, www.abc.net.au/news/2014-11-20/ clay-millennials-are-driving-the-shift-away-from-cars/5906406; Alexa Delbosc, 'Why are young Australians turning their back on the car?', *The Conversation*, 5 January 2016, http://theconversation. com/why-are-young-australians-turning-their-back-on-the-car-35468.

6   Ari Shapiro, 'IKEA executive on why the west has hit "peak stuff"', *All Things Considered*, NPR, 22 January 2016, www.npr.org/2016/01/ 22/464013718/ikea-executive-on-why-the-west-has-hit-peak-stuff.

7   John Rolfe, 'Car spare parts war: Motorists warned prices are being jacked up by as much as 1000 per cent', *Daily Telegraph*, 11 December 2016.

8   Gilles Roucolle and Marc Boilard, '3D printing is already starting to threaten the traditional spare parts supply chain', *Forbes*, 6 March 2017.

9   Virginia Scott Jenkins, *The Lawn: A History of an American Obsession* (Smithsonian Books, 1994).

10 Rich Martinez, 'Homeowner lawn care fertilization practices', Florida State University presentation, http://consensus.fsu.edu/fertilizer-task-force/powerpoints/Martinez_Fertilizer_TF_10-11-07.ppt; Francie Diep, 'Lawns vs. crops in the continental U.S.', *Scienceline*, 3 July 2011, http://scienceline.org/2011/07/lawns-vs-crops-in-the-continental-u-s/.

11 See Clive Hamilton and Richard Denniss, *Affluenza: When Too Much Is Never Enough*, (Allen and Unwin, 2005).

12 Andre Stephan and Robert Crawford, 'Size does matter: Australia's addiction to big houses is blowing the energy budget', *The Conversation*, 14 December 2016, http://theconversation.com/ size-does-matter-australias-addiction-to-big-houses-is-blowing-the-energy-budget-70271.

13 The 1947 and 1954 figures were averaged to get a 1950 figure. Australian Institute of Family Studies, 'Households in Australia source data', accessed 9 August 2017, https://aifs.gov.au/facts-and-figures/ households-australia/households-australia-source-data#size2011.

14 Converted from square feet to square metres. US Census, 'Media and average square feet of floor area in new single-family houses completed by location', accessed 9 August 2017, www.census.gov/const/C25Ann/ sftotalmedavgsqft.pdf.

15 Statista, 'Average number of people per household in the United States from 1960 to 2016', accessed 9 August 2017, www.statista.com/ statistics/183648/average-size-of-households-in-the-us.

16 Robert Whaples, 'Hours of work in U.S. history', EH.net, accessed 9 August 2017, https://eh.net/encyclopedia/hours-of-work-in-u-s-history.

17 Bruce Chapman and Kiatanantha Lounkaew, 'How many jobs is 23,510 really? Recasting the mining job loss debate', The Australia Institute report, 6 June 2011, www.tai.org.au/node/1732.

18 Robert J. Samuelson, 'Alan Greenspan's flawed analysis of the financial crisis', *Washington Post*, 22 March 2010, www.washingtonpost.com/wp-dyn/content/article/2010/03/21/AR2010032101707.html.

19 'Byron's whaling past', *Byron Shire News*, 26 May 2005, www.byronnews.com.au/news/apn-byrons-whaling/142630.

20 Gavin Weightman, *The Frozen Water Trade: How Ice from the Lakes of New England Kept the World Cool* (HarperCollins, 2001), p 178.

21 Gavin Weightman, *The Frozen Water Trade*, p 188.

22 See for example Federica Cocco, 'Most US manufacturing jobs lost to technology, not trade', *Financial Times*, 3 December 2016, www.ft.com/content/dec677c0-b7e6-11e6-ba85-95d1533d9a62.

23 Australian Bureau of Statistics, 'Employed persons by Industry sub-division of main job (ANZSIC) and Sex', *6291.0.55.003 – Labour Force, Australia, Detailed, Quarterly*, May 2017.

24 Office of the Chief Economist, *Resource and Energy Quarterly* March 2017 issue, https://industry.gov.au/Office-of-the-Chief-Economist/Publications/Pages/Resources-and-energy-quarterly.aspx#.

25 Queensland Department of State Development, 'Carmichael Coal Mine and Rail Project', 19 June 2017, www.statedevelopment.qld.gov.au/assessments-and-approvals/carmichael-coal-mine-and-rail-project.html.

26 Based on calculations in Chris Taylor, 'Joint Report to the Land Court of Queensland on 'Climate Change – Emissions', appendix 1, 22 December 2014 *(Adani Mining Pty Ltd [Adani] v Land Services of Coast and Country Inc & Ors)*, http://envlaw.com.au/wp-content/uploads/carmichael14.pdf.

27 Australian Bureau of Statistics, *6291.0.55.003 – Labour Force, Australia, Detailed, Quarterly*, May 2017; US Bureau of Labor Statistics, 'Civilian Employment Level [CE16OV]', retrieved from FRED, Federal Reserve Bank of St. Louis, https://fred.stlouisfed.org/series/CE16OV; Bureau of Labor Statistics, 'NAICS 212100 – Coal Mining', *National Industry-Specific Occupational Employment and Wage Estimates* May 2016, www.bls.gov/oes/current/naics4_212100.htm; UK Office for National Statistics, 'Workforce jobs by industry', *UK labour market: July 2017*, www.ons.gov.uk/employmentandlabourmarket/peopleinwork/employmentandemployeetypes/bulletins/uklabourmarket/july2017.

28 Bureau of Labor Statistics, 'Employees on nonfarm payrolls by industry sector and selected industry detail', Economic news release, 4 August 2017, www.bls.gov/news.release/empsit.t17.htm.

29   Stephen Edelstein, 'Porsche makes more money per car than Audi, Bentley, or Lamborghini', *Motor Authority*, 14 March 2014, www.motorauthority.com/news/1090892_porsche-makes-more-money-per-car-than-audi-bentley-or-lamborghini.

30   Henk Bekker, '2017 (Q1) France: Best-selling car manufacturers, brands and models', 3 April 2017, www.best-selling-cars.com/france/2017-q1-france-best-selling-car-manufacturers-brands-models; Renault, 'Clio features and specs', www.renault.com.au/vehicles/cars/clio/clio/features-specifications; Automobile Catalog, '2001 Ford (USA) Excursion 4WD', www.automobile-catalog.com/make/ford_usa/excursion/excursion/2001.html.

31   Tesla, 'Model S specifications', www.tesla.com/support/model-s-specifications; Teslarati, 'Tesla being eyed by big General Motors', 18 July 2013, www.teslarati.com/tesla-being-eyed-by-big-general-motors-gm/.

32   James Ayre, 'Global electric car sales surpasses half a million in 2015', *CleanTechnica*, 8 March 2016, https://cleantechnica.com/2016/03/08/global-electric-car-sales-surpasses-half-a-million-in-2015/; Mark Rogowsky, 'Tesla plans to rev up to 90,000 deliveries in 2016, trampling any bears in its way', *Forbes*, 10 February 2016; Syrah Resources, 'The emerging giant of graphite supply into the renewable energy industry', investor presentation, 13 December 2016, www.syrahresources.com.au/investors/downloads/406; 'Electric vehicles to be 35% of global new car sales by 2040', *Bloomberg New Energy Finance*, 25 February 2016, https://about.bnef.com/blog/electric-vehicles-to-be-35-of-global-new-car-sales-by-2040.

33   'Lithium ion batteries are now selling for under $140/KWh – New York hears on Benchmark World Tour 2017', *Benchmark Mineral Intelligence*, 15 May 2017, http://benchmarkminerals.com/lithium-ion-batteries-are-now-selling-for-under-140kwh-new-york-hears-on-benchmark-world-tour-2017.

34   See for example M.J. Brear, M. Jeppesen, D. Chattopadhyay, C. Manzie, T. Alpcan and R. Dargaville, 'Least cost, utility scale abatement from Australia's NEM (National Electricity Market) Part 2: Scenarios and policy implications', *Energy* (2006), https://arena.gov.au/assets/2017/06/Brear-Least-cost-abatement-part-2-published-version_1.pdf; Juan Jose Vidal-Amaro, Poul Alberg Ostergaard and Claudia Sheinbaum-Pardo, 'Optimal energy mix for transitioning from fossil fuels to renewable energy sources – The case

of the Mexican electricity system', *Applied Energy* vol. 150, 15 July 2015, www.sciencedirect.com/science/article/pii/S0306261915004353.

35   Kate Blanchfield, Nan Tian and Pieter D. Wezeman, 'Biggest military spenders', Stockholm International Peace Research Institute, accessed 9 August 2017, http://visuals.sipri.org/.

36   Sean McElwee, 'The income gap at the polls', *Politico Magazine*, 7 January 2015, http://www.politico.com/magazine/story/2015/01/income-gap-at-the-polls-113997.

37   Simon Kuznets, 'National Income, 1929–1932', National Bureau of Economic Research bulletin 49, 7 June 1934, www.nber.org/chapters/c2258.pdf.

38   Don Watson, *American Politics in the Time of Trump*, Quarterly Essay 63 (Black Inc., 2016).

39   Kristie Arslan, 'Five big myths about American small businesses', *HuffPost*, 24 May 2011, www.huffingtonpost.com/kristie-arslan/five-big-myths-about-amer_b_866118.html.

40   Grover Norquist, 'Conservative advocate', NPR, 25 May 2001, www.npr.org/templates/story/story.php?storyId=1123439.

41   The World Bank, 'Electric power consumption (kWh per capita)', http://data.worldbank.org/indicator/EG.USE.ELEC.KH.PC?locations=AU-US.

42   BP, 'Underpinning data, 1965–2016', *Statistical Review of World Energy 2017*, www.bp.com/en/global/corporate/energy-economics/statistical-review-of-world-energy.html.